Emotional Intellige

CW01429662

Boost Your E.I. To Improve Your Social Skills, Self-Awareness, Self-Discipline, Relationships, Success & Happiness In Life

Emily Porter

Table of Contents

The Key To Change

There's a curious phenomenon that always confused me until I learned more about *Emotional Intelligence*.

We're often told that IQ or Intelligent Quotient – how intelligent you are – is the most important factor for success. Simply put, the cleverer you are, the further you should go in life.

Sounds feasible in theory, but it doesn't appear to be true, does it? We all know people who are clever or book smart but who can't seem to hold it together in the real world. Perhaps they're socially inept, too caught up in their own heads or unable to deliver results as opposed to theory.

Chances are you know someone with a medium IQ who is doing so much better than those extra clever people around him or her. I know I do, many people in fact. How is that possible?

Would it surprise you to know that people with average IQs outperform those with the highest IQs 70% of the time? Yes, that much. It's a staggering statistic, isn't it?

Clearly, IQ isn't the be-all and end-all the theorists would like us to believe, so what is?

Let me introduce you to the concept of **Emotional Intelligence**, another *'kind of smart'*.

Emotional Intelligence – you may have also heard it described as EQ, Emotional Quotient – is the somewhat elusive element within ourselves that helps us to navigate our social world. It aids us in managing our emotions, motivating ourselves to success and encouraging connections with others.

It pushes us forwards and sets us apart. 90% of top performers, for instance, are thought to have high Emotional Intelligence.

Your EQ determines how well you can recognize and manage your own emotions and those of others around you, and how well you can use them to succeed.

As Daniel Goleman, the 'Godfather' of Emotional Intelligence, says: *"If your emotional abilities aren't in hand, if you don't have self-awareness, if you are not able to manage your distressing emotions, if you can't have empathy and have effective relationships, then no matter how smart you are, you are not going to get very far."*

Harsh, but fair Daniel.

Emotional Intelligence impacts every single aspect of our lives, from our home life, our marriages, our relationships with our children, to our work life, our leadership abilities, our friendships and more.

It's the man struggling to tell his wife and kids that he loves them. It's the manager at work who destroys morale because he is unable to empathize with the team. It's the woman blindsided by other people's emotions because she just can't read their body language. These are all examples of poor Emotional Intelligence.

Does any of this sound familiar? Let's hold up the honesty mirror and see if any of these situations apply to you...

Have you been passed over for promotion more than once? Do you feel sad or down a lot of the time, but can't explain why? Do you often feel inadequate, bitter or victimized? Are you frustrated by how easily other people can read emotions?

If I asked you to put a three-word sentence together starting with 'I feel...', could you do it? Have other people pointed out your lack of empathy, or complained that you are uncomfortable to be around? Do you find it near impossible to admit mistakes or express regret?

Crucially, is your lack of emotional awareness interfering with your life? Is it disrupting your marriage, damaging your relationship with your children, or holding you back at work?

If you answered yes to some, many or all these questions, please know that I'm not a psychic: I've just described someone with poor Emotional Intelligence. Which would be you, my friend.

Emotions are not just for Christmas; they are here to stay and need to be handled carefully.

Here's the good news: Emotional Intelligence *can* be learned. If you have a sneaking suspicion that you could benefit from improved sensitivity in this area, or your significant other has outright told you that you would, this book can help.

At the heart of Emotional Intelligence are a set of skills, and skills can be learned, practiced and improved upon.

You can learn how to improve your emotional awareness and control, plus learn how to recognize emotions in others. You can also learn how to self-motivate, develop empathy and improve your social skills.

Having a strong Emotional Intelligence can completely transform your life and personality. You can change from a glass half empty to a glass half full person, learn to embrace rather than fear change, and no longer let weakness hold you back.

This book will teach you the theory behind Emotional Intelligence and provide real-life tips and tricks to develop it for yourself. We'll consider how to boost your EQ to benefit your home life, your personal relationships, your work life and more.

You'll learn how to recognize body language; how to prevent your emotions from damaging your wellbeing and gain tips on how to persuade and influence people.

We'll examine how your own Emotional Intelligence can impact your children; you'll learn how to handle tough situations at work and at home, and how to recognize manipulation when you see it.

Did you know, for instance, that people can 'catch' negative feelings like they catch the flu?

And that's just the tip of the iceberg.

So, what are you waiting for?

It's time to jump right in and change your life for the better. Welcome to the first day of the rest of your Emotionally Intelligent life…

Chapter 1: What is Emotional Intelligence & Why Do You Need It?

Travis Bradberry, co-author of *Emotional Intelligence 2.0*, wrote in his Forbes blog: *"Emotional Intelligence is the other kind of smart"* and that's a good way to describe it.

It turns out that there is more than one kind of intelligence: we're no longer just limited to book smarts. I don't know about you, but that makes me extremely happy. I appreciate the brain power that nature gave me and like to think I use it well, but I have so much more to offer the world than my IQ alone.

A high IQ is still beneficial; it can open doors and gain you entry to the executives' lounge, for instance. But research shows that it's Emotional Intelligence that allows you to stay there, to move up the ladder and be worthy of the place that your IQ won for you. Likewise, Emotional Intelligence is a crucial factor in how successful your friendships and relationships will be.

But What Exactly is Emotional Intelligence?

First, let's take a quick history lesson. If we wanted to identify the very first theory of Emotional Intelligence, we could perhaps go as far back as Darwin, who postulated that emotional expression was vital to survival and adaptability.

Emotional Intelligence was given a name and theorized about to the masses in 1990, when psychologists John Mayer and Peter Salovey described EI as *"The ability to monitor one's own and others' feelings and emotions, to discriminate among them and to use the information to guide one's thinking and actions."*

Fourteen years later, Emotional Intelligence hit the mainstream after Daniel Goleman released his influential *What Makes a Leader?* article in the Harvard Business Review, arguing that Emotional Intelligence was even more important than IQ.

Since then, Emotional Intelligence or EQ has gone global. Many companies ask applicants applying for jobs to take EQ tests; you'll also find numerous EQ tests online. Schools in the U.S. now have courses on emotions, it has been mentioned in numerous television shows and cartoon strips, and the term is now recognized in several different languages, including German, Chinese, Korean and more.

The theory of Emotional Intelligence is the information we never knew we needed. It explains a curious fact: if IQ is so important, why do people with an average IQ do better 70% of the time than people with the highest IQs?

The answer is because of their stronger *Emotional Intelligence.*

Emotional Intelligence is the intangible something in each of us that helps us to read other people, to empathize with them, to react accordingly and steer our way through the sometimes rocky waters of social intricacies.

It is both the ability to recognize and manage our own emotions, and to recognize, understand and influence the emotions of others.

In his book **Emotional Intelligence – Why It Can Matter More than IQ**, Daniel Goleman gave us five elements to define EQ. We're going to talk about these in much more detail in chapter seven, but for now, let me briefly mention them. They are:

Self-awareness: This is the cornerstone of Emotional Intelligence, namely the ability to recognize an emotion as it happens. You need to recognize your emotions before you can start managing them.

Self-regulation: You may not be able to control when you experience your emotions, but there are techniques you can learn to regulate them, and to alleviate negative emotion. Learn to self-regulate your emotions and you can manage disruptive impulses, take responsibility for your reactions, handle change, be open to new ideas and maintain your own standards of integrity.

You use self-awareness and self-regulation together to be aware of your emotions and direct your behavior.

Motivation: Motivation is crucial for any goal, as is a positive attitude. If you can catch negative thoughts as they occur, you can learn to reframe them more positively, which will help with commitment, initiative, optimism and the drive for achievement.

Empathy: The better you are at identifying how others feel, the better you can understand them, anticipate and meet clients' needs, develop other people's abilities, read a group's power relationships and leverage them. Note that we have a whole chapter dedicated to the 'dark side of Emotional Intelligence (potential manipulation) coming up later in the book too.

Social skills: Strong interpersonal skills are tantamount to success in life and in your career, especially in a global economy. If you can understand, empathize and negotiate with others, you can influence them, inspire and guide (leadership), send clear messages, handle conflict management, nurture relationships and work well with others towards collective goals.

So, in short, strong Emotional Intelligence skills can make you:

- A stronger leader

- A more caring partner

- A better parent

- More successful at work

- More confident

- A better listener and friend

- More popular with others

And that's just the start of the list!

Don't just believe me, look at the evidence.

Emotional Intelligence as a Predictor of Success

According to EQ coaching service *TalentSmart*, who tested EI alongside 33 other workplace skills, Emotional Intelligence accounts for a full 58% of success in **ALL** types of jobs.

In contrast, most psychologists agree that IQ only accounts for between 10-25%.

Companies have started to give hopeful applicants EQ tests before hiring, while others have introduced EQ training programmes to the workplace.

Studies show that 90% of top performers at work are high in Emotional Intelligence. You can be a top performer with low EQ but it's rare. Some industries seem to accept lower EQ standards than others (the tech industry for instance), but most now recognize that it's a crucial factor in a productive workplace.

When I was starting out in my career, I worked for a middle manager who was exceptionally clever but lacked the *'softer touch'* shall we say. He was very socially awkward, so much so that if he met you in the lift on the way into work he wouldn't even talk to you, presumably because he didn't know what to say. If he met you out of work completely, he probably would have imploded.

He wasn't a bad guy; he tried to lead fairly, didn't show favoritism, simply expected everyone to get on with the job in the same manner that he did. He could solve complicated logistical issues with ease, and yet he could never understand that people had different desires and motivations, let alone how to deal with them.

He lacked any real form of Emotional Intelligence, which was unfortunate for a leader whose job relied on a productive team behind him. Slowly, over time, morale fell, and he had no idea how to improve it *(or possibly even recognize that it was an issue)*. People left, productivity stalled and in the end, he moved on *(or was pushed out, we were never quite sure)*.

Knowing what I know now, I suspect he was asked to leave. Not because he wasn't intelligent enough to do his job; he was one of the cleverest people I've ever met. But because he couldn't keep loyal people by his side or encourage them to perform to the best of their ability.

After all, it's hard to be loyal to a brick wall, and that's sometimes what dealing with people with no Emotional Intelligence can feel like. You don't want to be that person.

The Use Of Emotional Intelligence In The Real World

Hopefully, my story above illustrates that Emotional Intelligence isn't just a theory… it's a part of our lives day in and day out. It impacts practically everything we say and do **EVERY SINGLE DAY.**

Men, every time you listen to your wife and take her thoughts and feelings into account, you are demonstrating Emotional Intelligence. Well done. If you allow her to influence your decision making by considering the above, statistics show you are much more likely to have a happy lasting marriage.

In contrast, 81% of marriages will break down if men refuse to share power, says the Gottman Institute, which takes a research-based approach to relationships.

Think back to the last argument you had with your significant other. Did you put aside the anger to listen and acknowledge her complaints, as she hopefully did with yours? Or did you get defensive, hit back with criticism or contempt, and then stonewall her when she later tried to talk about it? Yes, it's like I was really there isn't it?

If you did the latter, you need some help with your Emotional Intelligence, my friend. Why does it matter? Because research proves that emotionally intelligent husbands are the key to a lasting happy marriage.

If instead you had turned off the television when she wanted to talk and chose 'we' over 'me', your relationship, sex life and everything between would have been stronger as a result. You would also make a better father by the way, one who isn't afraid to 'feel' and will teach his children the power of emotions.

'Only 35% of men are Emotionally Intelligent'

I'm not here to criticise men. The truth is that Emotional Intelligence is often harder for men than women, partly because of early conditioning as children. A 12-year study of 130 newlyweds by the Gottman Institute, for instance, concluded that only 35% of men are emotionally intelligent.

That's a shockingly low figure, and probably unfair to the sensitive men among us who feel deeply and respect emotions. But there's no getting away from the fact that men, some women too, struggle to utilize Emotional Intelligence as well as they could. It's probably one reason why you picked up this book, isn't it?

It could, and probably does, stem from childhood where boyhood games focus on winning, while girls' games tend to concentrate more on relationships and emotions.

If a boy hurts himself during a rough game of football, for instance, often he is side-lined, and the game continues. No room for emotion there. In contrast, girls' games are often relationship-based and will come to a halt if those relationships falter, only to start again once peace is restored.

Throughout their adolescence, boys too will often hear key stereotypical gender phrases, such as:

Suck it up

Don't cry

Be a man.

As the popular parenting book **Raising Cain: Protecting the Emotional Life of Boys** says, boys are shown that emotion leads to weakness and dominance leads to respect. Neither of these things is true, but it's no wonder that men grow up to become less emotionally aware.

But we can change that, because here's the good news... Emotional Intelligence can be learned.

How to Develop your Emotional Intelligence

Unlike IQ, your Emotional Intelligence can be developed. Think of your EQ as a set of skills which can be acquired, practiced and improved upon.

While your IQ is fixed – your intelligence represents your ability to learn, which is the same at 14 as it is at 40 – Emotional Intelligence is not.

It's true that some people are naturally more emotionally intelligent than others, but it is possible to develop better EQ skills, and this book intends to show you how. You'll find tips, hints and strategies for improving your Emotional Intelligence throughout this book, but especially in the second half.

All of which brings us on nicely to the neuroscience of Emotional Intelligence. You see, one of the reasons why EQ resonates with so many people in so many walks of life is because there is genuine scientific evidence to back it up. Science proves Emotional Intelligence exists, and even better, proves that it can be developed.

The Neuroscience of Emotional Intelligence

Emotional Intelligence has an actual physical source in the brain. We take in information from our primary senses *(sight, sound, taste, touch, smell)* which must travel to the front of the brain for processing (allowing us to think rationally about our experiences).

Before it reaches the front brain, however, it passes through the limbic system. This is the place where our emotions are generated, meaning that we have an emotional reaction to events before the rational mind can interpret them.

Early psychology models described human behavior as a series of stimuli and responses, but now we know that there are several stages that come between stimulus and response as mentioned above. A stimulus is filtered through our attitude, before being turned into feelings, emotions and thoughts. Our response to this is the outcome.

Our Emotional Intelligence therefore is dictated by the level of effective communication between the emotional and rational centres of the brain.

So far, so good, but the amazing thing about the brain is that it has an ability to change, a plasticity. The brain is constantly evolving and growing new connections as we learn new skills.

By learning new strategies to boost our Emotional Intelligence, we encourage the brain to form new neural pathways, where billions of microscopic neurons reach out to other cells to form a chain or a neural path. Once formed, it makes it easier to kick-start the same action in the future.

The limbic system learns by doing, so in order to turn intentions into positive future behavioral habits, you need to repeat, practice and repeat.

This is the foundation of habits, and if you train the brain by repeatedly using new strategies to boost your Emotional Intelligence, this will become a habit too.

Let's dig a little deeper into the neuroscience and look at particular aspects of Emotional Intelligence. Let's consider interpersonal intelligence (the ability to understand the motivation and desires of others) alongside intrapersonal intelligence (our awareness of ourselves).

In neuroscience, both are intimately linked because the brain circuitry that helps us to understand others is largely the same as that which enables us to be self-aware and think about ourselves.

Matthew Lieberman from UCLA theorizes in his book *Social: Why our Brains are Wired to Connect*, that our need to connect with others is even more fundamental than our need for food and shelter. As such, our brain is constantly using its spare time to learn about other people and how we relate to them. He postulates that we each spend 10,000 hours learning to make sense of other people and groups by the time that we are just ten years old.

That's a lot of information, but it's one thing to understand something and another to know how to put it into practice, which is where a lot of prior EQ work fails. Let me give you a real-life scenario.

Have you ever known what you should be doing, but didn't know how to put it into practice?

Perhaps you knew that you should console your upset colleague when she was crying on your shoulder after hearing some bad news, but you just didn't know how or where to begin. You tried your best, but really it just amounted to some rather awkward back patting, a colleague who didn't feel in the least bit comforted, and the desire to run away and avoid the situation altogether.

The reason for your poor response is because the ability to know something and the ability to do something come from different parts of the brain – the neocortex (knowing) and the doing (limbic region).

The good news is that if you learn strategies for Emotional Intelligence – and rehearse them every chance you get – the next time you're faced with an outpouring of emotion from a colleague you'll instinctively know how best to help. You'll both feel better as a result, I promise.

Learning Emotional Intelligence strategies doesn't just apply to adults. A child's brain is constantly evolving and learning, so teaching children to be more emotionally intelligent can help them learn how to handle disruptive impulses at an early age and benefit them in the future.

This book will provide such strategies, so please, do carry on reading!

Chapter 2: IQ versus EQ and why this could change your life

Someone very intelligent somewhere said: *"A high IQ will get you through school, a high EQ will get you through life."*

That, in a nutshell, is the difference between IQ and EQ (Emotional Intelligence). Your IQ is related to book smarts, your ability to learn and apply information to skills, your logical reasoning, your spatial and abstract thinking, to give some examples.

All of which will stand you in good stead at school (and possibly at certain times at work) but won't allow you to understand and express your own emotions, or deal with those of others. Indeed, people with low Emotional Intelligence often fail to recognize emotions and can struggle in group settings as a result.

If you're strong in Emotional Intelligence, you will, however, be able to identify, assess and control the emotions of yourself, of others and of groups. Your EQ determines how you treat people in your life and that interaction will demonstrate how well you can cope with pressure.

In an ideal world, we'd all have strong Emotional Intelligence skills *AND* a high IQ. Wouldn't that give us an edge? Of course, we can't all have everything we want – I'd kill for an hourglass figure, for instance, or the ability to do complicated mathematical equations in my head – but I don't have, and can't do, either.

IQ cannot predict EQ

Here's the thing: there is no known connection between your IQ and your Emotional Intelligence. IQ cannot be used to predict someone's EQ; you could be off the charts brainy and lack Emotional Intelligence. Likewise, as we've already discussed, many people with average intelligence do extremely well in life thanks to their superior EQ.

So, don't think if you score average on an IQ test that you can't do much better on an EQ test, because you can. Anyone can learn how to handle emotions ... and the Emotional Intelligence strategies that I will reveal later in this book will give you a great start.

I've been throwing the terms IQ and EQ or Emotional Intelligence around a lot already in this book, so let's put them head-to-head to really gain a better understanding of how they differ...

Terms used:
IQ = Intelligence Quotient

EQ = Emotional Quotient, aka Emotional Intelligence

Measures:
IQ: A score to assess general intelligence, derived from a standardised test. IQ measures reasoning ability and academic competency.

EQ: A person's social and emotional competency. The ability to identify, understand and control your own emotions, as well as the emotions of others

Used For...

IQ: To identify people with off-the-chart intelligence or gifted individuals, determine academic abilities or identify those with lower mental abilities or IQs who may face challenges and need additional help.

EQ: To identify leaders and strong team players. On the flip side, lack of EQ can also identify those people who work best alone, or who have social challenges

The Abilities of Each...

IQ: Strong ability to analyse, logical reasoning, word comprehension; implementing knowledge and information, abstract thought.

EQ: Ability to recognize and control own emotions, as well as to perceive, evaluate and control other people's emotions, using them to facilitate action and solution.

Best Use in the Workplace:

IQ: Research and development, analysis and logic, challenging tasks

EQ: Teamwork, collaboration, leadership, using initiative, working in some form of social service role.

Can We Improve Our IQ and Emotional Intelligence?

I touched on this in the last chapter, but it's worth examining in more detail here: why can we improve one sort of intelligence (emotional) but not another (IQ)?

IQ is an inborn ability, fixed from birth and not something that we can alter. That doesn't mean that we can't better ourselves, of course. We can learn new subjects, a new language perhaps, or study topics of interest. But while learning is never a wasted endeavor, it won't do anything to boost your IQ.

Your IQ isn't so much what you know, as it is your ability to learn it. And that's fixed throughout your whole life, illness or age-related issues aside. How well you can learn new information in your teenage years will still reflect how well you can learn it 20 years later. It won't miraculously improve or jump up by several IQ points.

Let me give you a caveat here: while you can't significantly alter your IQ, you can learn how to tap into its full potential via the use of brain foods, mental exercises, problem-solving techniques and more.

These will encourage you to think in different ways, ensuring you make the most of the intelligence that nature gave you.

So, while you won't necessarily be any brainier, you may be perceived as such because your brain will be firing on all cylinders (or neurons!).

In contrast, Emotional Intelligence isn't innate but a set of skills that we learn without even realizing it to begin with. A great deal of our Emotional Intelligence is influenced by our childhood, with our parents or significant others playing a part by encouraging sharing, thinking about others, urging cooperation etc....

Such is the belief in the ability to enhance Emotional Intelligence that there are games and toys available for children to develop EQ and classes in school for Social and Emotional Learning. Children with issues with Emotional Intelligence have been shown to do well in these classes, and to improve their EQ abilities.

Individuals with high-functioning autism or Asperger's often struggle with empathy – a major element of Emotional Intelligence – and have difficulty in recognizing and responding to other people's emotional states. Studies have shown that there is still the potential to improve empathy among these groups as well.

Likewise, as I touched on in our last chapter, women are naturally stronger at empathizing than men, scoring significantly higher on empathy tests in studies. And yet men can learn the skills associated with Emotional Intelligence and go on to become just as strong at EQ, if not stronger, than women.

Which is More Important – IQ or Emotional Intelligence?

This is the question that theorists have been arguing about ever since Emotional Intelligence was first defined in 1990: which is more important, or more valuable, EQ or IQ?

You would expect me to say Emotional Intelligence is more critical, wouldn't you, and you'd be right, but it would be remiss of me to point out that some people still believe IQ to be a better predictor of success and that Emotional Intelligence is overrated.

There you go, I've done my duty and mentioned it, and now I'm going to ignore it because I just don't believe it.

Don't get me wrong, IQ does still have an important part to play in many ways.

After all, the most intelligent chap who ever existed, with an estimated IQ of around 220, was Leonardo da Vinci. As an artist, scientist, engineer, architect and inventor, he made a pretty lasting impression on the world. As well as the Mona Lisa and The Last Supper, he invented, drew designs for, or conceived of, a flying machine, parachute, a helicopter, a fully animated robot, a revolving bridge, and many other inventions. All before 1519; he was a genuine genius.

Some of his inventions were wildly unpractical, while others were criticised as so until the science caught up to his imagination, waiting hundreds of years before they could be applied. So yes, there's something to be said for IQ.

But, there is also hard statistical and qualitative evidence to prove that people with high levels of Emotional Intelligence are much better equipped to do well in life and work.

Think about situations and people in your own immediate world. Daniel Goleman, described as the 'godfather of Emotional Intelligence', made a good point during an interview that resonated with me, and probably will with you too.

During a school reunion, he discovered that the most successful man in the room wasn't the cleverest or the hardest worker when in school as you might think. Instead, he was the 'nicest', the boy who knew how to make people feel comfortable around him.

Think of your own workplace because it's a common phenomenon. It is not always the most intelligent workers who receive raises or promotions. In truth, it's not always the best workers either. Instead, it's the men and women who have the best social and political nous at work.

You've probably noticed it; you may have even complained or grumbled about it, especially if you were one of the 'better' workers left behind. Perhaps you put it down to playing favorites, to the recipient being a 'yes' man or woman, to your company treating you unfairly. Chances are, however, that the beneficiary of that much-longed-for promotion knew something you didn't: the power of Emotional Intelligence and how to wield it.

Or as the slogan of the TIME magazine cover story in 1995 said: *'IQ gets you hired, but Emotional Intelligence (EQ) gets you promoted'*.

'People with high Emotional Intelligence earn more'

There's a reason that people with high Emotional Intelligence make nearly £22,000 MORE per year than their low EI-counterparts. They operate much better in the workplace. Every point increase in EI is estimated to add just short of £1,000 to an annual salary. This seems to apply in all industries, across the world and in people at all levels, according to TalentSmart.

Who can afford to turn that down?

The hard truth is that until you too can learn to operate with Emotional Intelligence, you may be overlooked, and your work and relationships will suffer.

Research backs up this observation. A 40-year longitudinal study of 450 boys from Sommerville, Massachusetts, two-thirds of which were from welfare families, one third with IQs below 90, concluded that IQ had little relation to success in life or in work. Instead, childhood 'emotional' abilities such as controlling emotions, handling frustrations and getting along with other people made the biggest difference and determined a person's success.

It makes perfect sense when you think of it. A person with high Emotional Intelligence can relate to others well, work better in a team and is more approachable. They tend to be more self-confident, trustworthy and generally more likable across the board, which often translates to improved productivity at work. There is even evidence to show that salesmen and women with higher EQ levels typically sell more than their low EQ-counterparts.

So, who are you going to promote? Someone who makes your life easier by running the team effectively and who boosts both morale and productivity, or their colleague who works better alone, has an impressive IQ but just can't seem to talk to people? There aren't many industries nowadays that are prepared to ignore the difference.

A lack of Emotional Intelligence will negatively influence your relationships as well, with friends, partners, loved ones and children. After all, no one ever left a partner or initiated a break-up because the other partner was too understanding or too supportive of their dreams and ambitions.

What Emotional Intelligence is Not…

Before we finish this chapter, it's probably wise to briefly discuss what Emotional Intelligence is not, as well as what it is.

Emotional Intelligence (EQ) is not simply…

- Being calm

- Demonstrating optimism

- Being agreeable

- The triumph of heart over head

It is also not…

Personality: Personality is not the same as EQ. Personality is hard-wired and doesn't change; it's our innate inclination towards introversion or extroversion. We may be able to learn tips and strategies to help us come out of our shells if we're shy, for instance, but no matter how good we are at it, our original inclination to stay out of the limelight never really goes away.

My brother used to be painfully shy as a child and worked hard to overcome it into adulthood. Now many of his 'newer' friends may never suspect the shy, nervous child he used to be, but as his sister, I still see it. When we walk into a room, he spends a few silent seconds sizing up the occupants, determining his comfort level, and putting his 'mask' on. Over the years, that mask has stayed on for longer or become easier to don, but at heart, he'd still rather be at home, with a small group of close friends, or allowed to fade into the background. Personality is stable throughout our life and helps to define us.

Emotional Intelligence is NOT the same as Social Intelligence

Here's a tricky one. Social intelligence is often confused with Emotional Intelligence, but it's subtly different. Think of EQ as the present, and the reading or understanding of immediate emotions or feelings. The mother who knows why her baby is crying, for instance, or the facial recognition that tells you the shy child at the party is too scared to talk to others *(I want to give my brother a hug now)*.

In contrast, social intelligence is more about the future. You use your knowledge of situations, social dynamics and interaction styles to predict the typical reactions of people and use it to avoid poor outcomes and encourage good ones. The employee who knows the best way to approach his boss with bad news, for instance, is using his or her social intelligence for success.

Perhaps your boss never wants to be approached with a problem but with a solution, for instance, and you adjust your behavior accordingly. Or you know how your wife will react when you tell her you must work late again, so you sandwich it between good news and dampen down the protest. It's survival in a way, the ability to interact successfully with others in numerous contexts.

Note that this is not quite the same as the social skills, or strong interpersonal skills, mentioned as a component in Emotional Intelligence. With Emotional Intelligence, you understand and empathize with people in real-time situations, helping to handle issues as they occur because you can recognize them in a person's body language, tone, facial expression or more.

Social Intelligence, on the other hand, uses your prior knowledge of social dynamics to predict how best to influence another person ahead of time, avoiding uncomfortable situations that EQ would typically handle.

The good news is that EQ and Social Intelligence can be used together to give you an even stronger position in the workplace, among friends, and with partners.

Chapter 3: Using The Three Main Models of Emotional Intelligence In Your Life

Over the last few years, debate has raged about Emotional Intelligence. What it is, how it can or should be used, when, and who can best wield it. The notion that there was another form of intelligence – one that could be superior to IQ – turned traditional accepted theory on its head.

It's not surprising, therefore, that there has been considerable controversy over its existence. And like any new academic theory, people have sought to quantify, qualify and adequately define it. None of which is straightforward with something as intangible as emotions and emotional theory.

Hence, we have the three main models of Emotional Intelligence, each an attempt by an EQ expert or practitioner to adequately capture the full essence of EQ.

Hopefully, I've done a good job explaining it all until now that there can't possibly be any confusion, but we'll be generous and let the best minds in the field have their say too!

Emotional Intelligence, after all, is such a wide-ranging feature of our lives that it's no wonder there are some differences of opinion.

A strong EQ can help us deal with everyday stresses, solve conflicts, excel at work, become a strong leader, be a good husband or wife and an equally superior parent. It drives our behavior and decision making and determines how well we communicate with others. There isn't any part of our family or professional life that it doesn't affect.

Each of the three main models of Emotional Intelligence is a bid to adequately describe such a phenomenon.

They are:

- The Ability Model

- The Mixed Model

- The Trait Model

Each model is slightly different and can be used effectively in particular situations, such as in hiring employees, leadership training and career choices.

Let's look at each and see which we prefer.

The Ability Model

As developed by Peter Salovey from Yale University and John Mayer from the University of New Hampshire, this is a popular choice for recruitment selection.

Mayer and Salovey consider Emotional Intelligence to be a cognitive ability which is separate from, but still associated with, general intelligence. According to the ability model, emotions are not simply responses to stimuli but useful sources of information to help us make sense of, and navigate, our social environment.

We each vary in our ability to process emotional information and use it to relate to a wider sense of cognition. This pragmatic approach claims that Emotional Intelligence comprises of four key abilities or branches.

1 - The ability to perceive emotion: You could say that emotional perception is the very first step towards Emotional Intelligence. Without the ability to recognize and identify your own emotions as well as the emotions of others, the rest of the ability model cannot be achieved. It also includes the use of non-verbal stimuli such as body language and facial expression to recognize the emotions of others, as well as stimuli indicating the emotion in art and landscapes.

2 - The ability to use emotion to facilitate thought: Picture a child who knows when his or her mother or father is in a good mood. Perhaps daddy has just got home from work, put his feet up and enjoyed his first post-work drink, or mummy has had a spare ten minutes to herself.

Perhaps little Tarquin has finally cleaned his room or passed an important spelling test and his parents are over the moon. And that's when Tarquin asks for permission to go on an overnight camping trip with his friends. In colloquial terms, that's striking while the iron is hot, and it shows that Tarquin, for all his untidy ways, knows how to use emotion to get his own way. He knew not to ask earlier, when dad was tired, and mum was harassed.

Tarquin instinctively understands how to use other people's emotions to achieve his desired outcome and considered them in his problem-solving.

Problem = how to get mummy and daddy to agree to his overnight camping trip.

Problem solving + emotions = ask them when they're in a good mood, happy with Tarquin and much more likely to be open to the idea.

Clever little Tarquin, already talented at Emotional Intelligence; he could be a Prime Minister in waiting.

3 - The ability to understand emotions: Many people can recognize basic facial expressions but fewer can appreciate the nuances of complex emotional relationships or recognize/ understand emotion language. If you are blessed with the ability to understand complex emotions or choose to learn how to do so, you'll understand why life changing events such as death or divorce, for instance, can cause conflicted emotions at the same time.

4 - The ability to manage emotions: The highest level in the ability model is the capacity to regulate emotions, again your own or another person's. At its worst, it is manipulating someone else's mood and making it work for you in a detrimental way, as we will discuss later in the book. It's not necessarily sinister, however.

I'm going to blow my own trumpet here and say I'm extremely accomplished at Emotional Intelligence. You wouldn't believe a word I said in this book otherwise, would you? I admit that I've used and managed other people's emotions to achieve my own desired ends, but I'd like to think I've done it in a positive way to help them too.

Take my employee, Claire. Claire was a new employee, eager to learn and had a lot of promise, but over the space of a month her outlook changed; she started to arrive late, her work slipped, and she sneaked away for several long conversations on her telephone at inopportune times.

As her supervisor, I had a choice: allow her to continue, which was no-go; issue a warning which I suspected wouldn't solve the problem or talk to her about whatever was bothering her. After watching and analyzing her behavior and body language, I suspected the issue was something emotional which was affecting her work.

I took her aside one day and talked to her about it, letting her know that she could tell me whatever was bothering her. I'm not the sort of boss who insists the personal should never interfere with work; it does and always will no matter how hard we try. We're not robots.

Eventually, she confessed that she and her husband were getting a divorce and were fighting over the kids. I offered her some personal time off. She refused, said she preferred to keep busy, so instead I found her a short-term project that allowed her to set her own hours, but also kept her busy. We had a few more meetings and pep talks after that: business first, followed by a personal catch up afterwards.

A few weeks later Claire, now a newly revitalized employee, thanked me for the help I gave her, even though it amounted to nothing more than a chat now and again.

She was happier and I 'cured' an ineffective employee, granted through what some would say was emotional manipulation. I met her emotional needs via pep talks, heart-to-hearts and a project all her own, and simultaneously achieved my own end zone. It was a 'win' for both of us. If you're interested, Claire and her husband managed to reconcile, and I believe are still together today.

Testing EQ via the Ability Model

The essence of the ability model is that Emotional Intelligence involves more thinking than intuition. As such, it makes sense that it can be significantly improved by learning the relevant skills.

The original and only test associated with the ability model is the *MSCEIT test*. The test seeks to identify a person's capabilities according to the four types of abilities identified in the model, using a cognitive-based approach but with emotional-based problems to solve.

The result of the test is measured against 'correct' answers determined by EQ practitioners and experts, or via consensus scoring, using a worldwide sample of respondents to predict social mores and patterns of behavior and comparing your results against them.

The idea is to provide an objective element to a subjective subject, helping to identify how well you would react given any emotional-laden situation.

Of course, as the critics point out, knowing how to respond to one situation doesn't mean you would react the same way in reality. You could say the test is better at determining your knowledge of emotions as opposed to your ability to perform tasks using that knowledge.

Best Use of the Ability Model: The ability model is a popular choice for recruitment selection or any situation which would benefit from an objective assessment of someone's EQ. Proponents argue that the MSCEIT test is more accurate than self-reporting alone and, as such, may weed out the positive but fake first impressions that people often want to give in interview or hiring situations.

Criticism of the Ability Model: Despite its popularity in a workplace setting, several studies have questioned the validity of the ability model after it failed to predict job performance. Other psychologists criticise its focus on the intellectual use of emotion.

Others still warn that the model is predisposed to Machiavellian tendencies.

Mixed Model

As developed by David Goleman, this model is often used in the corporate world.

It's probably fair to say that the most widely used theoretical models of Emotional Intelligence include the ability model above and the mixed model, as defined by David Goleman. The latter is my personal favorite, which is why I've already mentioned it in chapter one and will talk about it more again later in the book.

For now, I'll mention it briefly here so that we can compare, and consider which situations are best to adopt the mixed model.

David Goleman's five components of Emotional Intelligence, as I've already mentioned, include:

Self-Awareness: Recognising your own emotions and that of others, knowing your own strengths and weakness, goals, values and motivations. In the mixed model, this also includes recognizing your impact on others and using intuition to make decisions based on how they alter the emotions of the people around you.

Self-Regulation: You could call this self-control, the ability to recognize your own negative impulses and emotions – not as easy as it sounds – and redirecting them in a more purposeful way. To do so also demonstrates adaptability.

Motivation: According to the mixed model of Emotional Intelligence, a person with a high EQ should be able to successfully motivate themselves to achieve their goals. Note that under this model, such goals are not only pragmatic ones such as a promotion, a raise or a new job, but also include success for success's sake, and for achievement alone.

Empathy: Empathy takes sympathy to another level and shouldn't be confused with the lesser emotion. When you feel sympathy for someone, you tend to feel sorry or bad for them because of a problem they face but that's as far as sympathy takes you. When you practice empathy, however, you can personally identify with the other person (often known as *'putting yourself in their shoes'*) and consider their feelings when making decisions.

Social skills: Typically used in leadership or conflict management, the mixed model assumes that you will use your EQ skills to manage relationships with the people around you, to move them in the direction you want them to go. This doesn't have to be as Machiavellian as it sounds, though it certainly could be. In a day-to-day scenario, however, it could be as simple as a manager finding new ways to motivate a lacking employee or attempts to impress on a first date.

Think back to the last first date that you had. You may have chatted about your respective backgrounds, discussed art, cinema, (hopefully not the weather), tried to impress each other with your wit and sparkling personalities. Assuming you liked each other, you communicated your positive attributes in the hope of moving towards a second date. Essentially you moved the other person where you wanted them to go – to meet again.

If you did that without knowing too much about Emotional Intelligence, imagine how many more dates you could secure once you know more.

Best Use of Mixed Model: The mixed model of Emotional Intelligence defines EQ using skills and competencies that are not necessarily innate but can be learned and developed. This lends itself to leadership. As such, the mixed model is often used in the corporate world, helping to evaluate management potential. Executives or management consultants may evaluate potential hires or staff members to ascertain how well they perform on the mixed model, before making recommendations or offering training to improve EQ.

Measurement of the Mixed Model: The default measurement system for the mixed model of Emotional Intelligence is generally self-reporting questionnaire, alongside an external questionnaire carried out by an employer or supervisor. If the latter is not available, self-reporting is done alone, but is not generally considered as scientifically valid.

Criticism of the Mixed Model: The mixed model has been branded akin to 'pop psychology' by some critics, who believe it is not scientifically proven. Fans however point out that something should not be rejected or considered lacking simply because it is widely respected or popular. That said it is important to ensure that the person administering the report is a professional and not a layperson.

Proponents of the ability model criticise the mixed model for including aspects of personality which are not inherently emotion or intelligence-based, claiming it provides inaccurate data and does not appropriately measure Emotional Intelligence. Fans of the mixed model point out instead that EQ cannot be completely removed from personality.

The Trait Model of Emotional Intelligence

As developed by psychologist Konstantin Vasily Petrides, the Trait model comes into its own in career decisions.

The trait model of Emotional Intelligence offers a controversial way of looking at EQ, very different to the ability model. Creator Konstantin Vasily Petrides describes it as *'a constellation of emotional self-perceptions located at the lower levels of personality'.*

Have you spotted the controversial aspect yet? It's there front and center with the loaded words *'self-perceptions'.*

You see while the pragmatic ability model is focused on outwards results, the trait model is geared towards emotional self-perception. In short, it measures how individuals perceive their own emotions and abilities, which then influences their behavior. Once you can recognize and use your own emotions, the trait model assumes you will be well-placed to understand and regulate the emotions of the people around you.

Why is this so controversial, I hear you ask? OK, consider this. How do you scientifically measure a person's level of Emotional Intelligence when you're just evaluating their own perception of themselves? If someone believes they are adept at recognizing other people's emotions but they're clueless, how do you record that? Unless you're excellent at Emotional Intelligence you could easily overestimate your real abilities in this area.

The trait model is based wholly on the perceptions of an individual, with little to no objective measures included. As such, it is near impossible to apply any scientific or academic evaluation, making it difficult to prove or disprove.

*While other models use self-reporting tools as well, the trait model completely lacks any objective measures.

Proponents of the trait model, however, point out that its focus on self-perception is not so far from the overall definition of Emotional Intelligence.

Despite their differences, all EQ models come back to the same basic principles – the ability to recognize, understand and regulate your own emotions, and to recognize, understand and adapt to, or regulate, the emotions of others. These core elements are true for all models of Emotional Intelligence.

Perhaps one of the most compelling arguments for the trait model is that it recognizes that emotional responses or personality characteristics may be ideal under certain situations, but not advisable under other circumstances.

Someone great at their job because of their drive and motivation, for instance, may not make the best husband or parent if that motivation encourages him to put work first, to spend hours away from his family at weekends and evenings, to miss piano recitals and his son's football matches etc. His work may benefit, but his home life suffers.

The trait model doesn't necessarily advocate the idea that changing your EQ is important; its acceptance of adaptability means that it must accept that a person's EQ can be weak in some areas but exceptional in others. Unless a person demonstrates a personality disorder or unhealthy patterns, it doesn't advocate promoting certain characteristics over others.

Of course, this also means that trait theory offers little idea for development and sparse guidance on how to change negative traits. Some would argue that there is little point in measuring something if you can do nothing to improve it.

Measurement of the Trait Model: While the trait model acknowledges that a person's Emotional Intelligence can grow and change, it relies heavily on personality, which it believes is mostly ingrained. As such, it theorizes that a great deal of your EQ-related behavior comes from your automatic responses, as opposed to learned ones.

There's no real way to effectively measure Emotional Intelligence using the trait model without also having to perform a personality evaluation. The trait model relies so heavily on personality characteristics – such as adaptability, assertiveness, self-esteem, stress management, emotion perception, happiness, optimism and more – that you need to have the framework and knowledge of an individual's personality beforehand.

Criticism of the Trait Model: Critics argue that any EQ model should be based on cognitive-emotional ability, as opposed to personality, and as such claim the trait model doesn't effectively measure Emotional Intelligence. They point out that our own preferences, passions and biases filter how we see ourselves when interacting with others, which are bound to filter into our reports of self-perception.

Self-report is the most common way of measuring Emotional Intelligence under the trait framework, but it is notoriously unreliable.

Research proves that most people using self-report only relate their most recent or most intense emotional experiences. Memory-based self-reporting also isn't as accurate as objective accounts, with memory versions often over-estimating the reality.

Early EMA research on smoking, for instance, demonstrated that people often poorly recalled their quitting or smoking cessation day. They also overestimated their distress when quitting smoking in memory compared to their actual levels of distress recorded in real-time in an electronic diary.

Women also overestimated retrospective premenstrual symptoms relative to in-the-moment reports. Such overestimation after the fact has been demonstrated for a variety of emotions. Study participants rating their previous day overall, for instance, tended to recall more pleasant and unpleasant emotions than they reported feeling in real-time, with a greater emphasis on the unpleasant pain.

Self-reporting, therefore, can be unintentionally inaccurate, but there is also the ability to lie or stretch the truth.

Imagine you are taking a test for a potential job: are you going to be 100% truthful or would you, like most of us I imagine, 'stretch' the truth a little bit to make yourself look better? It doesn't even have to be a big lie, just a little white lie that will help convince prospective employers that you are the best man or woman for the job.

If you were going for a sales job, for instance, and were asked questions about your level of extroversion or introversion, how would you reply? If you are an introvert, would this go against you in a sales role?

I don't know about you, but I've known many salesmen and women, and they all have a few key traits in common: confidence, extroversion, and a refusal to accept the word *'no'* combined with the ability to talk the hind legs off a donkey.

If you're an introvert, you might be tempted to lie on the form just a little, perhaps answering yes to questions such as *'I prefer social activities to solitary ones'*. Sales work doesn't usually lend itself to curling up at home with a good book.

It's also true that while the model may identify where a person falls on a specific trait, i.e., at the high or low end, it cannot predict how they will act in different states. An introvert, for example, may be reserved in most situations but be outgoing with close friends.

For all these reasons, self-reporting alone is not considered a strong scientific measure.

Best Use of the Trait Model: Experts are split on the use of the trait model. Some argue that because it uses only self-report and no objective results, it shouldn't be used in a professional capacity, certainly not hiring or employment practices.

Where the trait model may come into its own, however, is its use in career determination. A great deal of research has gone into determining traits that are helpful to particular jobs, such as extrovert in sales and conscientiousness in teachers, for instance.

By measuring and matching a person's traits to others who are successful in a specific career, experts can determine which careers or college subjects should best fit their personality.

Chapter 4: Controlling The Role Emotions have on our Life

As Abhijit Naskar wrote in The Art of Neuroscience in Everything, *"You must know that too much emotional suppression can have a catastrophic impact over your body."*

Ignore your emotions at your peril because they will come back to haunt you, often physically. The man who never learns to deal with his anger, for instance, may be putting himself more at risk of a heart attack later down the line. The professional who can't find a way to adequately deal with the stress of the job may find themselves with a stomach ulcer.

Emotions have been proven to impact our physical and mental health. Let's face it, if you can't manage your emotions, you're probably not managing your stress particularly well either, which comes with a whole host of health problems. Uncontrolled emotions and stress can also cause mental health issues such as anxiety and depression. Being unable to understand and be comfortable with your own emotions makes forming relationships difficult, leaving you isolated and lonely.

Don't ever think that your emotions aren't important. They're so important that they can physically and psychologically affect our bodies: it doesn't become much more dramatic than that.

Strong Emotional Intelligence = Good Physical Health

This is where Emotional Intelligence comes in. After all, one of the main cornerstones of EQ is that we become aware of, and learn how to regulate, our emotions. Numerous studies demonstrate that higher levels of Emotional Intelligence are linked to better physical and psychological health. What's more, many of the studies were able to specify which EQ traits are the most significant when it comes to maintaining our health.

A 2001 Israeli study of EQ and physical health, for instance, determined that several Emotional Intelligence-related abilities *'significantly differentiate'* between healthy and unhealthy individuals. (* Study participants included 941 male conscripts to the Israeli Defence Forces with an average age of 18.)

Self-regard is the strongest predictor of good health

According to the study results, you should be healthier if you can:

- Manage emotions and cope with stress
- Adapt and be flexible to new situations
- Solve problems, both personal and interpersonal
- Work to realise and achieve your personal goals
- Be optimistic
- Be content with yourself, others and life in general.

Numerous other studies back up these findings. They demonstrate that self-regard *(your ability to understand and accept yourself)* is the strongest predictor of good health.

Alongside this – and no doubt the consequence of a positive self-regard – are other Emotional Intelligence-related factors that further boost your good health potential. They include a high tolerance against stress; self-actualisation (realizing and fulfilling your talents and potential); **optimism and happiness**.

All the above directly influence your physical state of health. Note too that your tolerance to stress and self-actualisation are also two of the most powerful Emotional Intelligence-related contributors to mental health as well as physical.

Studies Prove EQ Link to Poor Health

The results have been echoed in study after study. An investigation by the University of British Columbia in Vancouver into the link between Emotional Intelligence and alopecia patients found similar findings.

Participants with alopecia areata – an autoimmune disorder characterized by hair loss – were examined alongside randomly chosen non-clinical subjects. Results showed that the patients with alopecia experienced more difficulty in coping with stress and managing emotions, were more pessimistic and unhappy than the non-clinical subjects. They also demonstrated less self-awareness and a poorer self-acceptance and were less motivated to pursue their goals.

Note that the ability to manage emotions and combat stress was by far the biggest Emotional Intelligence deficiency among the alopecia patients when compared to healthy individuals.

Similar findings prove true for a South African study of coronary heart disease patients. 58 people were assessed for Emotional Intelligence within 10 days of being admitted to hospital post-heart attack and compared to a healthy group.

The findings indicated that the heart disease patients had significant deficiencies in their ability to manage emotions and stress; to solve personal (and interpersonal) problems; lacked flexibility and struggled to adapt; and appeared less motivated to pursue their personal goals than the control group. Perhaps because of the above, they were also less content with their lives and unhappier than the control group.

Are we Built for Stress?

Let's stop for a moment and consider one key 'deficiency' noticed in the above studies, and one that crops up time and time again. We mentioned it earlier. The ability to manage stress comes hand in hand with being unable to manage our emotions. Being unable to handle either can be a significant cause of mental, physical and behavioral problems in our lives.

We can't avoid stress; it's all around us in one form or another. Our bodies are even designed to experience stress and react to it. Some stress can be positive; consider the 'fight or flight' reflex which helps to keep us safe and avoid danger. Stress can be chronic or triggered by life events such as the death of a loved one, losing your job, a child leaving (or returning!) home, divorce or marriage, promotion, money problems, illness, moving to a new home and/ or having a baby.

An individual who cannot handle stress or who fails to gain any relief between stresses, however, risks a build-up of stress-related tension. You may notice this as agitation, moodiness, feeling overwhelmed, struggling to quiet your mind, low self-esteem, depression or a host of other emotional symptoms.

The stress also has a physical reaction as well, often quite a dramatic one. Stress can play a part in everything from headaches, raised blood pressure, heart problems, upset stomach, diabetes, and insomnia. Research suggests it can also make existing diseases or symptoms such as asthma and arthritis worse. It reduces the immune system making us more prone to frequent colds and infections, low energy, aches and pains, and more.

Mental health too suffers under relentless stress. You may experience constant worrying, forgetfulness, racing thoughts, poor judgment and struggles to focus, plus being pessimistic and unable to look on the positive side of things.

There's a reason stress, alongside anxiety and depression, is behind one of five visits to the GP, and around 9.9million working days are lost each year to all three.

'I could never switch off'

I know a little bit about stress. A decade ago, I oversaw a team of 50 people working around the clock, 60 if you also considered remote workers. I can't tell you exactly where as I don't want to shoot myself in the foot by offering too much information, but let's just say it was a high-pressured media-related role and there were a lot of eyes on me.

The job was so highly pressured we considered work in terms of minutes, not hours. I worked an average of a 12 to14 hour day with a two hour commute each way; looking back now, how I did it I'll never know. I was perpetually shattered.

I worked Monday to Friday and tried to regroup over the weekend *(for which read, sleep, sleep and sleep some more)*. All of which may have been doable if it hadn't been for the constant evening or weekend telephone calls from my team or my very demanding boss asking for help or advice, reminding me of something to do the next day, or just letting me know practically every thought that he had the second that he had it.

I could never switch off because I wasn't allowed to. I told myself that I was handling the stress well, and as crazy as it sounds it was true in some ways. I got to work on time, I was switched on from morning until night, nothing got past me, and I excelled at my job. On the surface of it, I was thriving.

But forgetting for a second that my social life was non-existent *(who had time, or the energy?!)*, my health wasn't so great either. My skin was blotchy and spotty *(an adult woman cast back to her teenage years)*, I suffered from lots of headaches and I drank so much coffee to get me through the day that my heart often seemed to race at night. My friendships and relationships too were all on hold *(and some never recovered)*.

Strange as it sounds, it took me a long time to realize that something was wrong. I honestly thought I was handling the stress and my challenging boss well and dealing with the emotions both brought. It was a lie, and it took me a bad illness where I couldn't even get out of bed, wiped out by a common virus because my body was just so exhausted, to realize it. If I wanted my life and my health back, I had to quit the stress, which is exactly what I did. Let me tell you, my physical health has improved dramatically since, as has my mental health.

By the way, a colleague who followed me into the role left too after six months because she'd started suffering from panic attacks for the first time in her life. Some things just shouldn't be tolerated.

The plus side of all this is that my near burnout was the instigating incident that led me to investigate Emotional Intelligence and a whole new line of work, and I'm happy to say that I haven't looked back since.

More than most, therefore, I'm aware that stress tolerance is intimately connected to our Emotional Intelligence. Being aware of and attuned to our moods helps us to cope with stress, as well as other potential health risks. Research also demonstrates that being EQ-savvy also helps us to overcome any hesitation in seeking medical attention, and we are much more likely to proactively seek solutions leading to better health.

All these behaviors are strongly linked to Emotional Intelligence, to an acceptance of personal reality and sense of accountability. In short, if you are self-aware, motivated and self-regulatory – all essential components of Emotional Intelligence – you are more likely to experience positive health outcomes.

We all deserve to be healthy, don't we?

Chapter 5: Why is Emotional Intelligence So Important?

We've reached chapter five and I hope already by now you have some sense of why Emotional Intelligence is so important. Let's do a little quiz to test your knowledge.

Is Emotional Intelligence important because:

- It's essential for a balanced life?

- It's critical for leadership?

- It determines how well you'll do in your job?

- You can make more money with a strong sense of EQ?

- It helps us to manage stress and keep physically and mentally well?

- It strengthens our marriages and relationships?

- It helps children to develop suitable peer relationships, reach their potential and develop a well-balanced outlook on life?

- All the above?

If you chose the latter – all the above – you'd be correct. Bit of a giveaway really, I know. But yes, Emotional Intelligence really can boost your success and happiness in all areas of your life.

I've thrown in quite a lot of impressive statistics into this book so far, all intended to demonstrate just how much Emotional Intelligence impacts your home life, marriage, children, relationships, work, leadership and more. Showing how a high EQ can work for you and, contrary, how a low EQ can work against you, often without you even knowing it.

Perhaps it's time to put all those statistics together on one page. When we see them in one list, it really does bring it home just how crucial our emotions, and our ability to manage them, are. I'll throw in a couple of new facts as well, just to make it interesting...

- 90% of Top Performers Have High EQs

- Emotional Intelligence is Responsible for 58% of your Job Performance

- People with a High EQ Make $29,000 More Per Year than their Low EQ Counterparts

- Every Point Increase in Emotional Intelligence is worth $1,300 more to an Annual Salary

- 71% of Hiring Managers Value EQ over IQ

- People with Average IQs Outperform People with High IQs 70% of the Time – Thanks to Emotional Intelligence

- 81% of Marriages Will Fail if Men Refuse to Share Power and Act with Emotional Intelligence

- Studies prove that self-regard (your ability to understand and accept yourself) is the strongest predictor of good health.

- People Prefer to Do Business with People They Like and Trust, even if Someone Else has a Better Product at a Cheaper Price

- A 1997 Study Proved that Sales Agents with High EQ Sold More than Twice the Insurance Policies of a Sales Agent with Lower EQ

Got the message yet?

There's a lot more I could add here, but I don't want to bamboozle you with too many facts and statistics. There's a lot of independent evidence that your level of Emotional Intelligence can improve your life significantly or hold you back just as much.

Let's take a deeper look at how it can do that, starting with the bigger picture.

EQ = Key to a Balanced Life

On a broader scale, Emotional Intelligence is crucial to building a balanced life. It's not only important for sales people or those who need to interact with others in their jobs; it's the gateway to a happy, healthy balanced life for all of us.

As you heard in our last chapter, until I quit my high-pressured job, I had no idea how out of balance my life was. My job success seemed to be the most important thing in my life; unfortunately, it ended up becoming practically the only thing in my life.

I want to believe women can have it all, men too for that matter, but to do so, I now believe you need to be attuned to your Emotional Intelligence, certainly more than I was at the time.

Since I left that job a decade ago, I'm now healthier and happier with a decent career and a family of my own. I firmly believe none of those things could have happened if I hadn't quit my job and learned all about Emotional Intelligence.

So, how balanced is your life? Let's take a quick sanity check, shall we?

How happy and content do you feel with all aspects of your life? Are you giving all your time and effort to just one part of it, or are you clear about your priorities?

I'm not just talking about time, of course. For most of us, work will always take up most of our day. But when you get home to the family, are you emotionally present? Do you switch off, and put the kids first? Do you plan activities with them on the weekends, for instance?

Is your physical and mental health strong, your wellbeing and outlook positive? Are you able to manage your stress in a healthy way? Do you communicate well with your significant other and consider them in your plans? Would they say that you do?

Lots of questions, I know … but it's worthwhile asking them of yourself and being honest with the answers. If you hesitated on any one of them, chances are your Emotional Intelligence might need a bit of work. And hey, the good news is that you're already reading this and that's what we're going to teach you in the second part of this book. You've taken the first step to a healthier balanced life already.

So, let's delve deeper and have a closer look at how Emotional Intelligence can help us to balance the different facets of our life.

Why is Emotional Intelligence So Important to Our Physical and Mental Health?

We pretty much covered this exhaustively in our last chapter but it's worth stressing again that the ability to take care of our bodies and to manage our stress is tied heavily to our Emotional Intelligence. Being aware of our emotions and our reaction to stress is the only way to adequately manage it and maintain good health.

Our Emotional Intelligence too affects our outlook on life and our attitude. A higher level of EQ correlates to a positive and happier outlook, helping to alleviate anxiety and avoid depression. As we know from our last chapter, anxiety, depression and negativity have been shown to contribute to physical ill health.

Why is Emotional Intelligence So Important to Our Relationships?

We're going to dedicate a whole chapter in the second half of this book to the role of Emotional Intelligence on our relationships, but needless to say, the success of a marriage or partnership is often determined by the partners' EQs.

Emotions can get confusing and conflicted in a relationship sometimes, can't they? There's often so much pressure to meet someone, move in together, get married, have kids, have a life together that we're not always 100% thrilled with it all 100% of the time. We're human beings, after all.

But if we want our meaningful relationships to flourish – and let's face it, at the end of the day they are what makes the world go around – we need to be better equipped to handle our emotions.

By understanding and managing our emotions, we can communicate in a more constructive way. No more flying off the handle or staying silent and stubborn for days after an argument.

Sound familiar? I promise I haven't been spying on your household; both are common reactions when we're not fully in tune with our emotions or haven't learned how best to communicate them yet.

Enjoying a strong Emotional Intelligence, however, helps us to understand and relate to those closest to us, and to appreciate their needs, feelings and responses.

A close friend of mine learned this the hard way. Married for ten years with two children, she thought she and her husband were on the same wavelength. They didn't always talk through their issues or share much alone time (often hard with kids), but she assumed he felt the same way she did. She thought they were building something meaningful together and life would get easier later down the line.

Another mutual friend of ours assumed the same about his wife, even though they too had some issues. She seemed to enjoy working more than she did being at home, but they were still mostly happy, or so he thought. He believed he was giving her the space she needed to find herself.

You can probably guess what's coming next. A tale as old as time, as the Beauty and the Beast song goes. Both spouses were wrong about the strength of their relationships and found out just how wrong they were when their respective other halves left them... for each other.

The cheating spouses had been having an affair for quite some time and when I spoke with them both alone, they said the same thing:

'we weren't happy in our marriage'. How can one partner be so unhappy and the other one not know it? It's a question cuckolded spouses no doubt ask all the time.

You could blame the partner left behind for not being emotionally intelligent enough to realize there was a problem, or to see it in the other's one's face, behavior, or body language, and it could be true. Alternatively, you could blame the cheating spouses for being inconsiderate and selfish, and hiding their true emotions.

But what I've noticed time and time again is that the people who leave marriages rarely do it on the spur of the moment. They've been unhappy, often considerably so, for quite some time. And yet, a lot of them have never discussed it with their spouse or tried to address the issues… they often haven't known how.

If they'd had better Emotional Intelligence, they would have been more in tune with their emotions and recognized how they were feeling earlier. They could then have tried to discuss it with their significant other, gone for couples' therapy and perhaps even saved their marriages and not ripped apart a family.

In the case of these two cheating spouses, it's fair to say they had weak Emotional Intelligence which led them to make poor choices. Those decisions cost them their relationships with their partners and with their children, who resented them for destroying two families.

In case you were wondering, their affair didn't last long once they left their respective partners either. Two people with low EQs don't help to form a healthy long-term relationship.

Why is Emotional Intelligence So Important to Conflict Resolution

Emotional Intelligence also comes into its own when it comes to conflict resolution. When you're able to discern other people's emotions and empathize with them or with their perspective, it's easier to resolve conflicts or avoid them before they even start.

Why is Emotional Intelligence So Important to Our Success

It sounds strange to say that Emotional Intelligence can help us to be successful but it's true, and there's proven evidence of it. It's quite simple when you consider how. Higher emotional intelligence gives us a stronger internal motivation, pushing aside procrastination, boosting our self-confidence and allowing us to focus on our goals.

Just as important, being emotionally intelligent and able to forge strong connections helps us to create a better network of support around ourselves, which can help us to overcome setbacks and be more resilient in our outlook.

The Consortium for Research on Emotional Intelligence in Organizations points out decades of academic investigation proves that EQ enhances satisfaction, goals, productivity and other aspects of our professional life.

Developing Leadership Skills in Life

I'm going to discuss the role of Emotional Intelligence on leadership and professional work later in chapter 10 in more depth, but it's worth mentioning it here in brief now.

As Daniel Goleman said, *"People do not leave the company, people leave bad bosses."*

Strong Emotional Intelligence gives us the ability to understand what motivates our staff and relate to them in a positive manner, helping to improve the bond. It's a misnomer that people are motivated by only money or recognition; motivation is much more complicated than that, driven from both the external and the internal. If, as a boss you can recognize a person's individual motivations, you can appeal to them in the most effective way.

An effective leader with strong EQ skills can also identify the needs of his people and address them in a way that boosts performance and workplace satisfaction. Recognising people's emotions can also help a talented leader build a strong team taking advantage of the emotional range of the people around him.

Our Children

It's fair to say that we learn a great deal of our Emotional Intelligence in childhood because of interaction with our parents. It can start early in our formative years where consoling a crying child, for instance, teaches them they can trust you and the world around them and helps to ease their anxiety.

The tone your family sets around emotions can influence a child and follow them into adulthood. If emotions are something to be denied or shameful, it becomes extremely difficult for a child to learn how to identify and manage their own emotions, or how to respond to others'. They are much more likely to try to hide or dampen down their emotions, meaning they will grow up to be adults with poor Emotional Intelligence.

According to child clinical psychologist, Dr Tali Shenfield, the best way to help your child to learn strong Emotional Intelligence skills is to accept and acknowledge their emotions, both positive and negative, and to empathize with them. Talking about their feelings, as opposed to trying to distract or deny them, teaches them that emotions are OK. Giving them time to process and manage their emotions and giving them the means to do so (such as giving them the words they need to express themselves) will help them to develop a strong Emotional Intelligence.

A strong EQ will help your son or daughter in childhood as well as later in adulthood.

Relationship guru *Dr. Jeffrey Bernstein* says EQ is a key predictor of a child's ability to forge peer relationships, to bond with his or her family, to reach academic potential at school and to develop a well-balanced outlook.

A child who scores high on EQ usually has an even nature and an accurate outlook of themselves. As they grow older, they can work through age-related challenges and recover from setbacks, either alone or with help. In short, they will become much happier and healthier individuals; what more could we want for our children?

Of course, it's hard to do all the above without strong Emotional Intelligence skills of your own and you may be worrying whether yours are good enough. We all worry at times about failing our children but as I have said before and will keep repeating, the good news is that Emotional Intelligence can be learned.

You can learn how to take control of your emotions, and this book will help you to do exactly that. First though, read ahead to the next chapter to learn the signs that tell you whether you have low Emotional Intelligence in the first place.

Chapter 6: How to Really Tell if You're Lacking in Emotional Intelligence & What To Do About It

You might be wondering why we need this chapter; surely, you'd know if you lack Emotional Intelligence? Do you really need a checklist to tell you that you could handle your emotions a little better?

Well, here's the ironic thing about EQ: If you do lack Emotional Intelligence you'll probably be the last person to realize it.

Your significant other will no doubt be aware of it, your colleagues and underlings will probably complain about it, and any children you have will, unfortunately, copy it. But you, my friend, may well be oblivious.

If you're lucky, someone will kindly point it out to you before it's too late, or you may hear it from a shocking 360 review at work.

If you don't realize it in time, you may find yourself missed over for promotion again as a result.

Let me tell you a true story. John *(not his real name)* believed he was at the top of his game at work, achieving results and meeting deadlines. In truth, he did have some impressive skills that encouraged clients to work with him in the first place. And yet, he was continually passed over for promotion at work. He started to believe the company was biased against him, possibly because the boss was scared he would one day take his job.

Of course, the truth was very different. As his colleagues and direct reports pointed out on a 360 review that HR instigated across the company, John's way of achieving success wasn't sustainable.

He was rude to clients without seeming to realize it; he belittled his team, was often impatient and lashed out if the work wasn't done to his exact specifications. His team had the highest turnover rate in the company.

While he 'pushed' his team to meet deadlines, he struggled to keep either underlings or clients happy; many of the latter never came back to him. Peers too didn't enjoy working with him.

For clients, the stress and hassle of delivery wasn't worth the end product, no matter how good it was. Other companies supplied equally, or nearly, as good products without the stress.

For his team members, being shouted and sworn at whenever John's temper flared – granted, a brief flame but a strong one – made work deeply unpleasant.

John thought nothing of the above, and assumed his team knew it was never personal but just 'his reaction' to stress, a flare up immediately forgotten with no hard feelings.

John was shocked when his 360 report highlighted his unacceptable behavior, both from his peers, his team members and his boss.

Tempted to reject it at first, he talked over his outrage with his wife – a woman, thankfully, of very high Emotional Intelligence – who knew all too clearly how John struggled with communication at times. She worked hard to tactfully encourage John to see the review as an opportunity. If he could work on the points raised in his review, he could finally earn that well-deserved promotion and they could start the family they'd always wanted.

During their discussions, John's wife also urged John to realize a very important fact – John's outbursts were the same as his father's before him, whose temper flared every time John did something wrong as a child. While never physical, John still used to hate those moments, and he was mortified that he had unknowingly copied such negative behavior. More than that, he was upset to realize how unhappy he had been making the people around him.

John wasn't a stupid man, just naturally low in Emotional Intelligence, but once he set his mind to it, he worked hard to tackle his issues, identify the triggers to his anger, and to find a more suitable outlet for it. He made a point of showing his appreciation to the team, backed off being so controlling and worked to turn around the negative attitude.

It wasn't a quick fix but over time team loyalty increased, productivity rose and 18 months after his first ever 360 review, John earned that promotion. Well done John.

Does any of John's story sound familiar to you? Do you treat people the same way John did? If so, you may struggle with low Emotional Intelligence, and the chances are that even if you are aware of it, you may not know how to improve it.

First thing's first: let's find out if you do have low EQ. Let's look at some signs or clues that show your Emotional Intelligence could do with some work.

A quick note here before we begin. As you read through the signs below, be honest with yourself. Do any of them sound like you, or would other people recognize you in the descriptions? If you're committed to improving your Emotional Intelligence, the first step is to be open to the fact that you have a problem and not to get defensive about it. That way we can work together to get you to where you want to be.

10 Signs that you have Low Emotional Intelligence Without Even Realizing

You Get Stressed Easily and Perform Poorly at Work

Everyone can have an off day, but if you lack Emotional Intelligence you may have more off days than on and perform consistently poorly at work. As we already know, 90% of top performers at work have high Emotional Intelligence; people with lower EQs can still perform well but it's more unlikely.

Take John's story above. He believed he was doing well at work, but he couldn't hold onto customers or workers for very long. He also got stressed very easily – a common sign of low Emotional Intelligence. Denying your feelings only helps them to build and escalate into tension, anxiety and stress.

Someone with better Emotional Intelligence would be able to spot tough situations earlier and head stress off at the pass, but if you lack EQ you're twice as likely to experience anxiety and depression, as well as to turn to substance abuse and even to think about suicide. As we already know, chronic stress can also play havoc with your health.

So, answer honestly: how well do you manage your stress? What techniques and de-stresses do you use? If you don't have any (or rely on unhealthy crutches such as alcohol) you need to carry on reading this book for the help you need.

You are Quick to Criticise and Blame Others

Being critical of others is never a constructive way forward, whether you do it to their faces or behind their backs as gossip. Finding fault is as far removed from empathy and Emotional Intelligence as you can get. Yes, constructive criticism is sometimes needed, but should be done privately and genuinely to improve someone's performance.

Likewise, if you blame all your relationship woes on someone else, for instance your partner, rather than taking your shame of the blame, it's likely that you're not very clued in to your Emotional Intelligence. Everything is not always someone else's fault and your attitude could be the essence of the problem.

Think of it this way: your emotions are your own, they come from within. No-one else can make you feel anything you don't want to. If you decide a negative 360 review, for instance, is an opportunity for change, it becomes a positive thing, and loses its power over you. It is no longer something to be upset about, and you no longer have any reason to be angry at the people pointing out your 'flaws' (which have now become opportunities for improvement).

Likewise, choosing to hold a grudge is just that, a choice. A negative one too, may I add. Holding a grudge is a stress response and even thinking about the reason for the grudge sends your body into fight-or-flight mode. That can be useful when faced with imminent danger, but when reacting to an old perceived threat, it plays havoc with your body. Holding onto stress contributes to heart disease and high blood pressure.

Blaming other people instead of taking responsibility for your emotions will only hold you back. Blaming your misfortune on others only stops you from seeking solutions yourself.

You Fail to Control Your Anger

Consider your actions today and be honest with yourself. How many times did you lose your temper today? If your temper flares often, it's a sign that you don't know how to manage your emotions.

It doesn't have to be a big flare-up, but consider how often other people's words irritate you? Do you feel offended if someone disagrees with you, no matter how politely? Do you dislike it if someone offers help when you haven't asked for it? When was the last time you uttered the words 'I'm surrounded by idiots'?

Or perhaps you tend to go the other way, and never show your anger. That can be equally as bad. Suppressing your emotions never ends well; sometimes it's important to show others that you're sad or upset or frustrated.

Masking your emotions or alternatively allowing them to run rampant means that you aren't dealing with them, and too much anger can have serious health effects later down the line.

You Have Difficulty Asserting Yourself

If you have a high EQ, you will be able to walk the fine line between asserting yourself and respecting boundaries and doing so with good manners and empathy. It's a tactful combination, perfect for preventing or handling conflict. You will remain balanced in the face of potentially toxic people, helping to neutralize difficult situations.

On the contrary, people with low Emotional Intelligence struggle to assert themselves effectively, because they resort to passive or aggressive behavior when tested. Their belligerent reaction will over-shine any attempt to be assertive.

Your trouble asserting yourself may also interfere with any attempt to work in, or lead, a team. Part of leadership – whether you are officially in charge or just a member of the team – is to communicate and persuade other people towards your purpose. That takes tact and the ability to manage your emotions. Otherwise, you risk riding roughshod over partners, friends, colleagues, and subordinates, abusing power and suffering from emotional outbursts. Trust me, you won't make friends and influence people that way.

You Don't Consider Other People's Feelings

Empathy is a particularly difficult emotion to master if you struggle with low Emotional Intelligence. If you are a manager, consider how you lead others. Are you approachable? Do people come to you with their concerns? Do you welcome feedback?

If you answered yes, that's great, but let's just sanity check it for a second. You believe you're sensitive to others and your door is always open, but when was the last time anyone took advantage of it? Can't remember? Chances are you're not quite as amenable as you think. The same probably also applies to your home life too.

Of course, being mindful of other people doesn't mean that you give in to each request that you receive. If you're the boss, or a supervisor, the buck may still lie with you, and you have a right to make the decision. A boss sensitive to EQ, however, will ensure his direct reports understand why the decision was made and help them to appreciate the situation, so that they can get behind it.

You Refuse to Leave Your Comfort Zone

Getting out of your comfort zone can be difficult for a variety of reasons, but people with low Emotional Intelligence are particularly loath to do anything new. They prefer their routines and patterns and don't like to be challenged by the unfamiliar, partly because it's difficult for them to process any new emotions that they may feel.

Part of those established routines, unfortunately, may be a penchant towards negativity. We all look on the negative side sometimes, but people with low EQ do it often and to their detriment. They cannot recognize their own emotions or comprehend that they are the cause of their current predicament, and thus fail to recognize that their thinking is clouded by their own bad mood or negativity.

Without recognizing this, they are unable to change it and negativity wins the day. People with low Emotional Intelligence, therefore, are more likely to give in to stress and anxiety and convince themselves that there is no hope.

You Give Up Easily

People may have told you that you give up too easily in the past or complained that you don't like adversity. That's certainly true of people with low Emotional Intelligence. People with low EQ would rather give up when faced with hardship so they don't have to face whatever issues crop up as a result.

Simply put, people with low Emotional Intelligence tend to be short sighted. They hope that by ignoring the issues or delaying having to face them, they will simply go away. In contrast those with high EQs know that's rarely true and overcoming them is healthier and better in the long run.

You Feel Misunderstood and Bitter

When you lack Emotional Intelligence, you may feel misunderstood by many because you aren't able to deliver your message in a way that other people can easily understand. It's easy to feel aggrieved when you don't get the reaction you want, especially when you don't understand how you come across to others. People with low EQ struggle to understand the reaction to their words, whereas those with higher EQs recognize that they occasionally need to adjust their approach and re-communicate.

When you feel misunderstood, it's easy to become bitter, but let me tell you something that will hopefully stop you in your stead. If you're bitter about your failures, you are likely to be bitter about other people's successes too. Why did they succeed where you failed? It's just not fair!

Does that sound like the sort of person you want to be? The type of person you want your child to learn from? I hope you answered 'no' to both of those questions.

Being bitter about yourself and others is not a nice place to be, and chances are the bitterness you feel at your failures is out of proportion to the success or progress you're already making.

You see, people with low Emotional Intelligence tend to focus on the negative, as I've already said, which means that you're much more likely to concentrate all your attention on the 'failures' or things you haven't yet achieved, than on everything that you have. Your frustrations are magnified, and you forget to be grateful for the things you do have or should be celebrating.

Don't forget the famous saying from the man described as America's greatest inventor, Thomas Edison: *"I haven't failed. I've just found 10,000 ways that don't work."*

His never-give-up attitude brought us the lightbulb, worldwide power, the phonograph and more than 1,000 other patents, many for items still in use in some format today. Imagine if he'd suffered from low EQ and gave up at the first hurdle? How much worse off would the world be today?

You Never Want to Appear Wrong

Do you like to argue, even if there's no point? Perhaps it would be best to agree to disagree, but you just can't let it go. That's typical of someone with low Emotional Intelligence; you just can't get over your ego. You never want to appear wrong, even though everyone is at some point. You'd even allow the situation to become awkward by refusing to play fair because you must 'win'.

If you make assumptions quickly and refuse to back down when challenged, even politely, chances are you need to work on your Emotional Intelligence. This is particularly dangerous in a management situation as ill-thought out ideas can end up team strategy.

You Don't Recognize your Triggers

Everyone has triggers – situations or people who get under their skin and cause them to act rashly and without thought. If you're strong in Emotional Intelligence, you learn how to recognize and sidestep your triggers, avoiding the car crash results. If you're low in EQ, however, you may not even be aware of them and the results will be the same each time.

As part of this, you may be easily offended. It's hard for truly Emotionally Intelligent people to be so easily offended. They're confident in themselves and open-minded, meaning they usually have a thicker skin. As such, they don't allow people to pierce that confidence.

You, however, may take offense at the slightest thing, unaware that you are being 'triggered'. Likewise, if you don't recognize the triggers, events, people or subjects, that cause you to lose your temper time and time again, you won't be able to prevent it. And as I said above, being angry all the time is not a nice way to live.

If you see yourself in any of the above, don't despair! As I've said time and again in this book, Emotional Intelligence can be improved. You can learn how to handle your emotions, and how to appreciate and recognize them in others.

Read on for part two of this book and the help you need. We've covered the theory, now we're going to talk about the practical. You'll find part two chock full of hints, tips and practical advice on how to tackle your low EQ and work your way to becoming a better husband, wife, parent, friend, manager, leader, colleague and all-round better person.

You'll learn how to train your brain by repeating and practicing new Emotionally Intelligent behavior, creating the new pathways you need to turn your actions into habits. Before long, you'll begin to act with high EQ without even thinking about it, and your old destructive behavior will be far behind you. Read on! Part Two awaits…

Part 2

Chapter 7: The 5 Most Important Qualities of EI… and How to Gain Them Fast!

Dale Carnegie has some words for us to live by as we try to master our Emotional Intelligence.

He said: *'When dealing with people, remember you are not dealing with creatures of logic, but with creatures of emotion.'*

Our feelings are what drive us forward, forge our relationships, encourage our success at work… or equally, hold us back. They are the primal force, our instinct, which is why it is so important to learn how to control them.

I always think of the perceptive quote by Greek philosopher Epictetus here.

"Any person capable of angering you becomes your master; he can anger you only when you permit yourself to be disturbed by him."

I find it an inspiring quote to remember; it reminds me that we have the power to decide how to feel. We don't have to feel anxious, negative or fearful, or rather we can choose how to react to incidents which would typically cause those same emotions and steer them in a different direction.

Welcome to the second half of this book, the section where we really look at how to improve your Emotional Intelligence. We're not just talking theory anymore. The pages from here on out are loaded with practical advice, tips and ideas for improving every aspect of your EQ.

I promise it won't be too painful. You will just need an open-mind, the willingness to change and the patience to really look at yourself and see how your emotions are affecting your behavior and influencing the people around you, for good or bad.

It will take a great deal of introspection, a big dollop of brutal honesty and a calm, clear mind. So, stop whatever else you're doing – multitasking isn't a plus here, you need single laser-like focus – and get ready to change your life.

You'd be well advised not to miss any of the following chapters as they are relevant to your relationships with your nearest and dearest, work colleagues, friends, acquaintances, peers and underlings alike... in short, to every single aspect of your life.

If you commit to, and practice, the steps listed in the rest of this book, you will become a popular, empathetic and well-balanced person, someone people will want to work for and to be around. It takes on average 66 days for a new behavior to become a habit, so before long acting according to positive EQ principles will become second nature.

We're going to start by looking again at David Goleman's Mixed Model of Emotional Intelligence and identify the five most important qualities needed for EQ. We'll look at typical traits exhibited by people with high Emotional Intelligence and show you how to get them for yourself.

According to the Mixed Model, the five components of Emotional Intelligence are:

- **Self-Awareness**

- **Self-Regulation**

- **Motivation**

- **Empathy**

- **Social Skills**

Let's look at how you can achieve each skill. Make a note of that word – *skill*. That's what each of these components is, a skill, and it's exactly why it's possible to learn and improve Emotional Intelligence. It's never too late.

Let's begin!

Self-Awareness

Let's look at how to be aware of your emotions and the emotions of others.

Individuals with emotional self-awareness often have the following traits:

- They can recognize which emotions they feel and why

- They appreciate the link between their feelings and their behavior (what they say, think and do).

- They recognize how their emotions influence their performance

- They are aware of their values and goals and keep them in mind to guide them.

How do some people achieve this level of self-awareness? They are happy to gain feedback, learn from experience, have perspective on themselves, are continuously learning and are open to self-development.

There's another element to self-awareness under **Goleman's Mixed Model**... being able to recognize the emotions of others and appreciating how your emotions and behavior impacts on them. So, we can add the following traits to the previous list:

- They can recognize the emotions of other people around them

- They realize how their feelings impact on those people

- They can use intuition to make decisions and influence the emotions of the people they want to 'sway'.

Self-awareness may be just the first step in Emotional Intelligence, but it lays the foundation for the rest of your EQ. If you fail to be aware of your feelings, you will never be able to control them, or to be aware of others' emotions around you.

Self-Awareness

As I've said many times in this book, it is possible to learn to be self-aware and to develop awareness of your emotions. In doing so, it becomes easier to recognize the emotions of the people around you, and to appreciate how your feelings impact on them.

With that in mind, however, you may find it a little difficult to begin with. It can be hard to recognize and catalogue more than one emotion at once and you may struggle if your emotions change from one minute to the next. Perhaps your early life encouraged you to distance yourself from emotions, particularly common if your emotional experiences were painful, frightening or confusing. If so, you will have to work through that mental block.

It is also common for people to be in denial about certain emotions such as anger and fear, believing they demonstrate weakness.

I say this not to dissuade you, but to forewarn you. If you appreciate that being self-aware takes work and may not come easily straight away, you will be less likely to give up if the going gets tough. You'd make Billy Ocean proud. I do, however, have full confidence that you can learn how to be self-aware and learn how to recognize and appreciate your emotions for the powerhouses they are.

So, where to begin? Let's look at some practical strategies.

Manage Stress

If you haven't yet learned how to manage your stress, it's imperative to do so first. Emotions are heightened under stress and if you can't handle the latter, chances are you will struggle to have the mental capacity you need to calmly identify your emotions during a taxing incident. Of course, the irony is that's probably when you need to keep track of your emotions and, subsequently, control your reactions the most.

When you learn to manage stress, however, you will feel more comfortable experiencing strong or unpleasant emotions and will naturally change the way that you respond to them.

Entire books have been written on managing stress and I can't do it justice within this one chapter alone, so I'm not going to say much more on stress here. Just know that there is a lot of light (and some not so light) reading around on the topic of stress if you need it.

Set the Mood

I'm not talking about soft candlelight and romantic music here, but more setting your mental stage. Picture an upset child; he or she isn't going to learn anything in the classroom if they are unable to concentrate or focus because they're upset about something. We may be taller, bigger and have a fair few pounds on our children, but the same applies to our mental state even in adulthood. Self-awareness benefits most from an enriching mood, allowing us to process our emotions.

As Goleman says, negative moods tend to reduce our ability to make sound decisions, to stay on task and focus. They also encourage pessimism, which may well be the emotional trigger you want to eliminate.

Try to set the mood first. A positive mood helps to boost creativity, improve problem-solving, decision making and mental flexibility.

Slow Down to Observe your Feelings

The key to being self-aware is to be able to observe and identify your emotions. The trick to doing that is to slow down. It's easy to lose touch with our emotions when we're busy or worrying about the next deadline, which is why we ignore them a lot. Being genuinely self-aware only works if you take the time to examine your emotions as they happen, rather than push them aside.

Suppressing our emotions only makes everything worse… from our relationships and work life to our health and well-being. Think back to chapter four – we learned that negative emotions can cause all sorts of ill-health, from high blood pressure to heart disease and more. Avoiding negative emotions can also encourage excessive behavior, from too much TV watching or game playing to self-destructive behavior with drugs and alcohol.

The more we avoid our feelings the more power they have over us and the more uncontrollable they become.

When you next feel a strong emotion, slow down, calm down and examine it. Think about why you are experiencing this feeling; strong negative emotions, for instance, are often due to unresolved issues.

Remember too that while you cannot choose what emotions to experience or when, you can choose how to react to them.

Keep a Journal

When you notice yourself feeling a strong emotion, the best way to deal with it is to write it down. The act of making a record often helps you to slow down, as mentioned above, and can help to take the sting out of an unpleasant situation by making you think logically and dispassionately about it. In turn, you give yourself more breathing time before reacting.

It has the added benefit of helping to identify patterns and potential triggers which can be seen when you look back over the week's journal.

Spending just a few minutes each day writing down your thoughts can, therefore, help you to move to a higher level of self-awareness. If you don't have a lot of time, create a form of shorthand for yourself.

If you feel silly writing a journal *(and there's no reason you should)*, consider it this way: everyone is appraised and observed in some way for their role at work, this is the same but on a more personal level. It really is worth taking the time.

What to Write in your Journal:

To get the most out of your journal, you'll want to make a note of the right sort of things to identify patterns of behavior and emotional triggers. The journal isn't the same as a diary: it's not a place to rant or rave at the latest indignity. If you do it right, it should force you to look at your emotions on an objective level instead.

As a good rule of thumb, make a note of the following:

- Who you interacted with and how they relate to you (i.e., work colleague, boss, husband, wife, July from accounting).

- What you discussed and how it made you feel.

- Consider your emotions for a moment and write down how strongly you felt the emotions above and if you could control them.

- Write down incidents where things went well and those that could have gone better. Doing so allows you to identify any key differences that altered the outcome to learn for the future. Constructive and objective criticism can also boost your self-confidence.

When you look back at your log of emotions, see if you can start to see any patterns. Do certain people wind you up, time and time again? Do certain topics make you feel anxious or negative? If you can identify triggers, you can create an action plan to handle them when they crop up again, as you'll find out in our next section on self-control.

If you are not sure where to start, begin with those incidents where you experienced negative emotions and reacted badly, i.e., with passive aggression, playing the victim, inappropriate humor, sarcasm or more. These are usually a result of anger, unresolved issues or avoiding confrontation.

How To Know Your Own Emotions

According to EQ coaching service **TalentSmart**, only 36% of people can correctly label their own emotions as they experience them. This may be partly due to a poor emotional vocabulary. You may describe yourself in your journal as feeling *'bad'*, for instance, while emotionally intelligent people will go further and pinpoint whether they feel *'anxious'*, *'frustrated'* or *'irritated'*.

Why is a strong emotional vocabulary important? Because unlabelled emotions are often misunderstood and can cause irrational reactions and counterproductive behavior. Truly understanding your emotions is a vital step before controlling them, and the more specifically you can label them, the more insight you have into them.

Ask for Feedback

Yes, this one might be a little bit painful, but put your ego aside and ask for feedback from others, whether during a 360 assessment or by asking other people what they observe about you. It's often the easiest way to find out how you behave around others. Before you go this route, make sure you are prepared to listen to the feedback and own it. There's no point if you're going to be defensive about it.

If you're honestly prepared to deal with the *'harsh truth'*, you will find it an extremely helpful tool in developing your Emotional Intelligence.

Once you can recognize, identify and understand your own emotions, it will be easier to recognize them in others as well.

Self-Regulation and Self-Control

Self-regulation or control is the second component of the Mixed Model and people with this skill usually demonstrate the following traits:

- They can manage impulsive feelings and distressing emotions

- They are focused under pressure and think clearly

- They remain composed and positive even in difficult situations

- They can build trust in others through their authenticity and reliability

- They find it easier to admit to their own mistakes

- They take tough stands on issues they believe in even if such a stance is unpopular.

How do such people achieve all the above? It helps if they are organized, flexible, prepared to take risks and to entertain original solutions to issues, as well as being accountable and committed.

Doesn't sound like you? Maybe not right now, but by the time you learn all there is to know about Emotional Intelligence and put your learning into practice, it may be.

Here's the one key fact to hold onto: **While we may not be able to dictate when we feel strong emotions such as anger or fear, or choose how strongly we feel them, we can decide what to do and how to behave while experiencing them. That gives us quite a lot of power over our feelings.**

In his book *'A Force for Good: The Dalai Lama's Vision for Our World'*, Daniel Goleman talks about intriguing research at Columbia University. Researchers studied volunteers who were exposed to photographs of people's faces demonstrating strong emotions. The volunteers relevant emotional centers of the brain immediately activated, for instance when they saw a woman crying or a baby laughing. Showing how instinctive our emotional reaction is.

But then the volunteers, led by neuroscientist *Kevin Ochsner*, were asked to rethink what could be going on in the more disturbing photographs. Perhaps the woman crying was at a wedding, for instance, and they were tears of happiness not sadness.

The intriguing thing here is that, while the volunteers pondered alternative situations for the photographs, the emotional centers of their brains lost energy while others in the prefrontal cortex activated instead. This suggests that using the prefrontal cortex more when faced with strong emotions can help to reduce our more primal reaction to them.

What does this mean for you? In a nutshell, it means that reasoning with yourself about your negative emotions and impulses can reduce your instinctive reaction to them, thus allowing you to control them.

Let's have a look how you can do that, and any other techniques that may help you to control your emotional responses.

Recast Your Emotions

The Columbia University example above essentially taught volunteers how to recast their feelings. While you may not be able to control when you experience your emotions, you can choose to try to see the situation in a more positive light; we call this 'recasting'.

Assume a negative incident has occurred that would typically have you losing the plot. Instead of reacting to it instinctively as you normally would, take the time to think about it instead. Look for a different way of viewing the same event, one that doesn't make you feel sad, scared, angry or anxious at the end of it.

If the boss has rejected the report you slaved over all night to complete, for instance, you may feel like shouting or yelling, or at least slamming a door or two. Perhaps you'd typically take it out on your secretary or direct reports; pass the frustration further down the line. It's not a side of yourself that you're particularly proud of, but if you're honest with yourself, it does happen.

But stop! Before you allow any of those emotions to take hold, try to consider the news in a different light. Yes, it's disheartening to have your work rejected, but it would give you the opportunity to add in those figures that came in after the report was submitted. They would strengthen your case significantly. Perhaps you could also seek further clarification on the results of the test you quoted from R&D. You must admit the evidence was a bit thin there.

In fact, you have been given an opportunity – a chance to do the work better this time and to really impress your boss. This is your big break, the opening you need to finally win him over. Suddenly what threatened to ruin your day has morphed into a new challenge, and the emotions surrounding it aren't negative anymore. Well done, you have just recast your feelings.

Let's consider another example. Kyle had just started his new job and wanted to establish himself as a top-notch chef before he and his girlfriend tried for a family. After all, they had very little money, no house of their own and they were only in their early 20s; not exactly in the best position to be parents.

Or that was the plan until Cindy suddenly announced she was pregnant without warning – and they'd been so careful! Suddenly all of Kyle's meticulously crafted plans came crashing down. How could they look after a child with no money and no home? And how could Kyle be a father and still spend the time he needed to learn his trade and forge his reputation? Needless to say, he didn't take the news well.

"I'm a bit ashamed of that actually," a bashful Kyle admitted to me. *"When Cindy told me, my first thought was 'No!' I felt absolute fear. I wasn't ready to be a dad, and unfortunately, I told her so. I just couldn't see beyond everything we would have to give up."*

His relationship with Cindy – and possibly with his future child – very nearly broke up as a result until he came to me. I worked with Kyle to help him recast his emotions around the potential birth of his first child.

Rather than concentrating on everything he would potentially lose, I asked him to think about all the things he would gain – all the pleasures of fatherhood, of family. I had him paint a virtual picture of all the things he would enjoy, trying to make it as specific as possible.

When he mentioned his fears around work, I suggested he consider the satisfaction of achieving success for his baby boy or girl and being able to provide for them. Slowly he started to recast his emotions naturally.

Whereas before he had been frustrated because having a baby and another expense meant they would have to live at his mother's for longer, now he could see a positive side. Staying there would allow them to save a significant amount of money on rent or mortgage, helping them to save a deposit for their own place in their own time – and they would have an adoring grandmother and babysitter on hand 24/7! What a comfort to two first time parents.

I'm happy to say that Kyle and Cindy welcomed baby Esme into their lives shortly after, and she is the apple of both their eyes.

Develop Your Code of Ethics in Life

Know where you draw the line

One of the most effective ways to control your behavior is to have a clear idea of your values and ethics and appreciate where you absolutely draw the line. Take some time to understand what is most important to you and you probably won't need to think twice when faced with an ethical decision – you'll make the right choice because it will feel like the only one to make in your heart.

Be Accountable

Remember we talked about blaming others in the previous chapter, pointing it out as a sign of low Emotional Intelligence. If you make a point of holding yourself accountable and be prepared to admit your mistakes, whatever they are, you will not only earn respect from other people but probably sleep better at night as well.

Respond, Don't React: Create an Action Plan

We're all guilty of reacting to events at times, acting in an unconscious way because of our emotions, usually to express or relieve them. Such as the time you shouted at the junior on the team because he messed up the coffee order. Well, you really needed that caffeine!

The mocha latte you requested wasn't really the problem. It just masked the disappointment, guilt and anger you felt (and didn't know how to control) when the boss changed the management meeting and you had to tell your daughter that you couldn't make her music recital after all.

The key to self-regulation, however, is to respond (carefully and in a well-thought out way) rather than simply react (hollering every stress that you have, every second that you have it). It's a conscious process that needs you to pay close attention to your feelings and recognize emotional triggers, so you can decide how to react in a similar situation again.

Essentially, you need to learn how to pause. When you feel strong emotions, take two pauses: the first to listen to yourself. Learn to recognize physical responses to your anger, such as your jaw and hands clenching, and take the pause whenever you feel it happening. Remind yourself that you don't want to lose control and determine how you want to respond instead of lashing out.

Secondly, take a pause to make sure you listen to others. Active listening is so important, and pausing will give the other person the time to get their message across before you jump in. Even better, they will also believe that you have given them the respect that they deserve.

To make sure you can do this moving forward, it's a good idea to create an action plan to hold yourself to it.

This action plan will pull together the two elements of Emotional Intelligence that we've talked about so far – self-awareness and self-control.

How to Create an Action Plan

Step 1: Choose an incident to review, ideally something that you feel could have gone better.

Step 2: Examine the feelings involved, both your own and the other party's emotions. What emotions did you or they display?

Step 3: Consider if, and how, your emotions influenced the outcome.

Step 4: If you can recognize that your emotions shaped the outcome of the incident under review, you need to decide if it was for the better or not. Did they improve the situation or, more likely, interfere? Did they divert you from your objective or cause heightened emotions in the other person?

Step 5: What would you change if you could do it all again? What would you do differently, or do less or more of? How will you control your emotions?

Step 6: Now that you have a list of the changes you want to make to your behavior and the way you display your emotions, it's time to create your action plan. It should have clear and defined objectives, ideally short-term ones to begin with that focus primarily on your reactions, alongside specific tasks and a timeframe. Make sure you also give yourself time to review those tasks and make any revisions you need.

Let's look at how that might go.

Step 1: Caramel is creating her action plan and has chosen her *'inciting incident'* – the time she lost her temper when the Head of Sales blamed her department for poor annual sales in front of the MD. That meeting could have gone better.

Step 2: Caramel closely examined her feelings of the incident and realized that while she thought her strongest emotion was anger, there was also a great deal of concern underneath. What did the MD think of her after that? And could it be true; was her department lacklustre? What if she wasn't up to the job? It was hard enough to get the job in the first place in a typically man's world. At the same time, she recognized that sales were trying to head off criticism of their own department and were lashing out.

Step 3: Oh yes, her emotions influenced the outcome. Caramel acted defensively and aggressively, refusing to let sales continue their spiel. The meeting broke up shortly after, to be reconvened when everyone had calmed down a little. In fact, did she ever really let the sales director explain what he meant? No, she didn't.

Step 4: Upon close examination, Caramel is forced to admit her emotions interfered with the meeting's objective. They never did work out why annual sales were significantly down this year. She believes her department created a must-have in this year's hot new product, so why weren't people buying it? She still doesn't have any answers.

Step 5: What would she change if she could do it again? The main thing would be to stay calm and allow the sales director to finish his presentation. In the calm light of day, she can accept that he may have some insight that she doesn't have. She will try to control her emotions by remembering that everyone is in this together and the lack of sales affects everyone in the company.

Step 6: Caramel has created her action plan.

Her first few objectives were: Stay calm, manage stress, actively listen, and be accountable.

Her tasks included: Research how to actively listen. Manage stress by taking a walk around the block now and again. Practice deep-breathing exercises to calm down. Recast emotions by considering other people's role in the lack of sales, recognize their concern too. Be accountable by researching what people are saying about their new product online, to learn what the issues are and if it is poor design to learn from it.

Be sure to revise and revisit your action plan frequently to ensure it is still working for you.

Consider Your Words Carefully

When you have weak Emotional Intelligence, it's very easy to underestimate the effect your words can have on someone else. Without meaning to, you can put someone down, demoralize them, or make them bristle… and you probably have no idea you're doing it.

Nigel, a middle manager, used to do this often. He threw out words and phrases meaning one thing and was shocked when he discovered people took his comments differently.

Take for example his go-to 'morale booster'… *'If I can do it, anyone can'*. Nigel truly believed he was being encouraging by using the phrase, demonstrating that he was one of the team.

Unfortunately, his team begged to differ. Instead, when he said, *'If I can do it, anyone can'* they heard *'You're not clever enough to do this'* or *'If you can't do this, don't come to me because I won't be impressed.'*

This is the gap between intent and impact, and it's something you can learn to be aware of. Have you ever been guilty of saying something along the lines of *'I don't see what the big deal is'?*

What did you mean by that? Were you perhaps trying to placate someone, or even admit that you couldn't see why something was a problem? I can tell you how the people around you probably took it. They probably heard *'I don't care what you think'* instead. Yes, really. Phrases such as the two above are rarely taken at face value but come loaded with hidden meanings.

So, the rule here is to be aware of intent versus impact and to think carefully about the words and phrases you use because they too can have power. Consider the impression you want to portray about yourself and how you should frame your message to achieve it.

Now let's move onto the third component of the Mixed Model of Emotional Intelligence; motivation.

More Motivation In Life

'Nothing is impossible, the word itself says "I'm possible!'
Audrey Hepburn

The third element of Goleman's Mixed Model of Emotional Intelligence is motivation, the 'doing' part of the equation.

Remember the statistic I quoted at the beginning of this book? I pointed out that a staggering 90% of top performers are Emotionally Intelligent, an indicator that equates EQ with success. More than a little of that triumph comes down to strong self-motivation and the desire to achieve, something people high in EQ tend to have in spades.

The theory is that anyone with a high EQ should be able to motivate themselves to chase and achieve their goals. After all, they already know how to regulate their emotions to create a positive outlook and banish pessimism. If you can catch and reframe negative thoughts as they happen, for instance, you are much more likely to be optimistic and committed, both of which directly contribute to motivation. You'll also find it easier to maintain drive in the face of obstacles and challenges.

People who are self-motivated often demonstrate the following traits:

- They are results-oriented and ready to seize initiative and opportunities

- They are driven to meet their standards and objectives

- They aren't afraid to set challenging goals and to take calculated risks to achieve them

- They will persist in chasing their goals despite setbacks

A quick note here – under the mixed model, goals aren't limited to pragmatic desires such as a new job or promotion, or a raise. They also include success for the sense of achievement alone, doing something to prove to yourself that you can.

In a nutshell, self-motivation comprises our inner drive to succeed and commit to our goals, our optimism and our readiness to take advantage of opportunities. Considering setbacks as learning opportunities and surrounding yourself with positive people will do wonders for your internal motivation, as will identifying and setting goals for yourself.

Goal Setting for Motivation

Picture your goals as a roadmap. If you don't set goals for yourself, how will you know your desired destination? How will you get there? It's all too easy to lose heart and motivation if you haven't got a plan to follow.

I create goals in my daily life, even if it's just a list of things I want to do today. It could be something as significant as finishing the next chapter of a book (this one is on my list today!), or as mundane as cleaning the bathroom, changing the bed sheets or doing another load of washing. I don't need to write them all down; I'm more than capable of remembering them, but I write them down so that I can tick them off my list when I've done it. A visual representation of achievement.

Yes, I know the bathroom will only need to be cleaned again later and the sheets changed – and the washing is a daily occurrence at our house – but to cross them off my list gives me a sense of achievement and shows me that I have done something. It helps to foster my motivation.

It's even more important to have goals when it comes to the bigger things you want to achieve in life. Imagine you have a strong career goal – perhaps you plan to be a hospital consultant in 10 years or you want to run your own magazine. Maybe you want to become a top-notch ad executive, or you just want to earn a certain amount of money by the time you are 30, 40 or 50 years' old.

All well and good, but exactly how can you achieve that? How do you make sure that every step you take on the training or career ladder will lead you to that end? And how do you make sure that you don't go off track, get distracted or lose motivation along the way? After all, it's likely to be a long time in the future before any of this happens.

'Whether you think you can or you think you can't, you're right.'
Henry Ford

That's where writing down your goals and creating a plan comes into its own. Having a thought-out list of goals, broken down into milestones, works wonders for your motivation. If you ever find yourself worrying whether you can achieve the success you want, you can look at your goal plan and see exactly where you are. You can see at a glance all the success you have achieved so far, or, if the plan is not working, tweak it and start anew with renewed enthusiasm.

Setting goals helps to give you long-term vision and short-term motivation.

Play It SMART

Of course, it all relies on establishing intelligent and achievable goals. That's called playing it SMART. In a nutshell, your goals should be:

S – Specific
M – Measurable
A – Attainable
R – Realistic
T – Time-based and trackable

Let's have a look at **SMART** goals and goal planning in a bit more detail.

How to Set Personal Goals

Sitting down to plan and set your personal goals for the future can seem daunting, but it doesn't need to be. Follow these simple steps and they will almost write themselves.

Step One: Identify your Lifetime or Longer-Term Goals

Let's jump right in and think about what you want to achieve for the future. Try to create a 'big picture' of your goals, ambitions and dreams over the next 10 years for instance.

What level would you like to reach in your career, for instance, and by when? How much do you want to earn, and by what stage in your career? Do you need any further education to achieve your goals in this area? Do you want to be a parent, and how will you be the best parent you can be?

Are there any personal issues or attitude problems holding you back that you want to work on for the future? Do you have any physical goals, whether it's to lose weight, get fit or stay healthy into old age? Do you want to own your own home, for instance, or give back to the community at large in some way? If so, how?

Ensure balance by considering different elements of your life such as career, family, financial, education, physical, personal/ pleasure, artistic, attitude…any area that seems relevant to your personal circumstances.

Remember to keep your goals **SMART**. It's no good saying you want to be rich, for instance, if you can't specify how to get rich in a measurable, realistic, or attainable way. Take some time to carefully consider these goals as they will be the basis of everything that comes next.

Consider one or two goals in each category before trimming them down to a small number of significant goals that really matter to you. I'm stressing that, because it's all too easy to fall into the trap of choosing goals because your parents, significant other, employers or family want them; make sure the goals you choose resonate with you. *(Of course, you can take other people's wishes into consideration as well; your wife or husband should have a say in your future too).*

Well done. Now that you have your bigger picture, let's break it down into smaller manageable goals.

Step Two: Break your Goals into Smaller Targets.

Once you have your larger goals, now is the time to break them down into smaller targets. Consider what you will need to achieve before you can reach your lifetime goals. If you want to be a magazine editor, for instance, you presumably would first need to become a deputy editor (or move into an equally credible position for promotion to the top job). How can you achieve that? Would it be beneficial to move into a more niche subject area, for instance, or do you need any specific training to become a senior member of the team? How would you get that training?

Shorten your goals each time. Start by planning your goals for five years ahead, making sure it feeds directly into your longer-term goal (deputy editor, for instance) –, then two years or next year, next month, next week, day-to-day… The key is that each of these shorter goals should move you towards your larger goal in some way.

Each plan should be based on the one before to ensure they all help you move towards your bigger goal.

You may find that your short immediate goals are research-based, needed to gather information on how to achieve your longer-term goals (arrange an appointment with the current editor of the magazine, for instance, to learn more about the job/ qualifications needed). Filter this into your plan as well. While you are crafting your plans, keep SMART goals in mind and make sure the plans will fit into the kind of life you want to lead.

Tips for Staying on Course:

- Review your to-do lists on a regular basis, and your longer-term plans periodically, modifying them if you need to.

- If you have several goals, list them in order of priority and direct your attention to the most important ones.

- Keep your immediate and low-level goals small, achievable and incremental to make the best use of motivation. Anything too large and it can seem as if you are lacking in progress.

- Ensure the goals you choose are in your own hands. The best way to do this is to focus on performance, not outcome. That way, if you fail to achieve something because the outcome was out of your hands, you will know that you still achieved your performance target.

- When you achieve a goal, take the time to enjoy the satisfaction and build self-confidence. Learn from how hard it was to achieve: too long and you should make the next goal a little easier, too easy and you should make the next one harder. Decide whether anything you learnt while achieving that goal should influence your future goals and modify accordingly. Failing to meet a goal can be a learning curve too.

- Step out of your comfort zone. Sometimes the best motivation comes from challenging yourself to do something beyond what you normally would.

- Keep learning. Lifelong learning helps to feed the mind and keep it curious and motivated.

Empathy

Now it's time to move on to the fourth component of Emotional Intelligence; empathy. Before we look at how you can improve your empathy skills, there's a little fable that I love to repeat that sums up empathy far more effectively than I probably can…

Two seriously ill men shared a hospital room. One of the men had to lie completely flat on his back, while the other could sit up for an hour a day to have his lungs drained. The second man's bed was under the only window in the room and he spent the hour staring outside.

The men chatted endlessly about their families, their wives, where they had been on holiday and their jobs.

One day the man who couldn't move asked the other 'what can you see out of that window?' His roommate described everything he could see vividly, describing a beautiful park with ruby red flowers, emerald green grass and a lake. Ducks swam, children ran about, lovers held hands, with the city skyline as the backdrop.

As he described everything in detail, the other man would close his eyes and picture the scene. One day the man described a passing parade, the next an impromptu marriage proposal among the flowers.

Days and weeks passed, and the man looked forward to those one-hour periods where his roommate would eloquently describe life outside the window.

Unfortunately, one day the nurse came and discovered the man by the window had passed away silently in his sleep. The other man grieved for his roommate, but after an appropriate time had passed, he asked if he could move to the bed under the window. He really looked forward to finally being able to see the park, the lake and the flowers for himself.

It took a long time, but the man finally managed to find enough strength to rearrange his pillows and prop himself up so that he could get his first look out of the window. And when he did, he saw... a blank wall.

Shocked, the man asked the nurse why his roommate had made up such elaborate and exquisite stories about life outside the window, when there was just a blank wall.

The nurse shrugged and revealed that the man was blind and couldn't even see the wall.

She said: "Perhaps he just wanted to encourage you."

Wow, it's a powerful story, isn't it? It is also one that symbolizes empathy perfectly. The dead man had no motive for telling his stories other than to make the other man, bedridden and unable to move, happier for an hour each day. He understood how important it was that the other man heard about life outside his hospital room. He demonstrated empathy.

People with empathy usually demonstrate the following traits:

- They pick up on emotional cues and listen well

- They demonstrate sensitivity

- They understand other people's perspectives

- They offer help based on the other person's emotions and needs

Empathy takes sympathy to another level and shouldn't be confused with the lesser emotion. When you feel sympathy for someone, you tend to feel sorry or bad for them because of a problem they face but that's as far as sympathy takes you. When you practice empathy, however, you can personally identify with the other person and consider their feelings when making decisions.

The following quote from the **Gallop Business Journal** describes people with empathy as able to sense and understand the emotions of people around them;

'You can feel what they are feeling as though their feelings are your own. Intuitively, you are able to see the world through their eyes and share their perspective. You do not necessarily agree with each person's perspective. You do not necessarily feel pity for each person's predicament — this would be sympathy, not Empathy. You do not necessarily condone the choices each person makes, but you do understand.'

Empathy is an important part of Emotional Intelligence precisely because it can be so powerful. Someone with strong empathy skills will draw others to them. They will anticipate need before it is asked, will always seem to find the right tone and help the people around them express their feelings.

Recognising how people feel can help your success in life and career. Empathetic people are particularly skilled in service, being able to anticipate and meet clients' needs. They are also very strong at developing others and helping them to progress; skilled at reading a group's power relationships and emotional undertows, and leading others, earning respect by demonstrating that they care.

In short, being empathetic will improve your communication, resolve conflicts, boost your negotiation skills and make you a more influential person.

It's a valuable life skill, one that helps navigate and develop relationships, and if it doesn't come naturally to you, don't worry: it can be nurtured.

How to Practice Empathy

Active Listening

As Stephen Covey says in his book, **The 7 Habits of Highly Effective People**, one of the most important qualities needed for empathy is the ability to actively listen to the other person, to seek to understand before you seek to be understood.

Active listening is harder than it sounds. It demands 100% focus and the self-control to let the other person talk without interruption; you will need to put your own preconceptions, scepticism and issues to one side to absorb their situation. You will also need to learn how to avoid mental and environmental distractions.

To demonstrate empathy, you must do the above and consider how they feel before you react. When you do, you should acknowledge the speaker's entire message – reflect on what he or she has said to prove you were listening – before giving an honest and objective response.

The speaker will then feel that you have truly listened to them and be drawn to you for your empathy skills.

Open Up

Another way to demonstrate empathy is to listen to someone's experiences and relate it to a similar experience of your own.

Opening yourself up and offering a sincere exchange can prove to someone that you really can understand where they are coming from.

It's just one reason why the *#MeToo* movement coming out of Hollywood was so powerful; it connected women standing up against sexual assault and harassment via an inbuilt statement of empathy. Millions of women empathized with each other over the sexual harassment or assault they experienced, and by tweeting or posting the #MeToo hashtag, stood up for each other in an unprecedented way.

As activist **Tarana Burke** told CNN: *"It's a statement from survivor to survivor that says, 'I see you, I hear you, I understand you and I'm here for you or I get it."*

Facebook reported that in less than 24 hours after the *#MeToo* hashtag started trending, it had been used by more than 4.7 million people around the world in more than 12 million posts. More than 45% of people in the U.S. were friends with people who posted a #MeToo hashtag message.

Empathy really *can* change the world.

Change Perspective

You've no doubt heard the phrase *'walk a mile in someone else's shoes'*. It's an admonition not to judge someone until you've walked in their shoes or been in their situation. It's a warning that you can't appreciate the challenges someone else faces until you've either faced them yourself or put/ imagined yourself in their position.

So how can you do that? It's a matter of changing your perspective, from your own to theirs, to look at things from a different angle.

NLP – Neuro Linguistic Programming – has a whole model dedicated to just that, the 'Perceptual Positions' or 'multiple perspectives' model which helps to foster empathy. It sounds daunting, but it's really just common sense.

The idea is that by putting yourself in someone else's shoes or looking at a situation from their point of view rather than your own, you may learn new information or come to appreciate their feelings and actions, even if you don't agree or condone them. Let's have a quick look at the NLP model and how we can use it to help boost our empathy.

The Multiple Perspectives Model

NLP describes three main perceptual positions (if the terms bother you, think of them as different ways of looking at a situation) –

First position: Your own perspective, likely your default viewpoint. This is your sense of self, how you naturally perceive your environment. You look at things through your own eyes, hear with your own ears and feel your emotions in your body. It feeds into your sense of identity and enables you to be assertive, to pursue your own goals and to express your thoughts.

Note, however, that only ever operating from this position would make you insensitive, narcissistic and egotistical, not caring about the feelings of others.

Second position: This is the viewpoint from another person, which you may take on during certain interactions. It's the 'stepping into someone else's shoes' perspective, where you try to think as if you were them, to imagine their reality. You disassociate from your own thoughts and beliefs and see through their eyes. As you do so, you increase your awareness of what things might be like for them. This is a useful process to develop empathy, and to help you understand why someone behaves or reacts the way they do.

Note that getting stuck in this second position and always putting other people first can leave you emotionally drained and unable to fulfill your potential, as well as damaging your own confidence.

Third position: From a detached viewpoint, as an observer. People who can look at issues from the third perspective can benefit from the objectivity, ensuring their emotions don't get in the way during particularly awkward situations. As if they were a fly on the wall, they can feel and hear what an interaction is like from an external position and observe the relationship between themselves and others.

It seems obvious that a mixture of these positions, certainly positions one and two, would be beneficial for our relationships. As I said above, only ever considering things from your own perspective can make you insensitive to other people's feelings and egotistical. Sometimes imagining how the other person must feel, appreciating their thoughts and feelings and reacting with that in mind, can do wonders for friendships, marriages, colleagues and more.

If you're not naturally an empathetic person, try the following exercise.

Empathy Exercise

Consider a recent issue that you had with another person, whether at home, at work, at the pub or anywhere else. It could have been an argument or a disagreement, or even a time when someone around you did something you didn't expect.

Start small, don't try to fix the big issues in your life before you can walk. This is a work in progress.

Think about the incident mentioned above from your own perspective. Recreate it in your mind, experience it again through your eyes, hear yourself talk, hear the other person, notice how you reacted and recreate the feelings you experienced. Got it? Then step out of position one and take a break for a moment. Think of something different – what will you have for dinner tonight, for instance? (This pause is known as a break state).

Now it's time to switch to position two – the other person's viewpoint. Consider the situation completely from their point of view. What did they see or hear, what did they feel, what did they think to themselves, think as if you were the other person. It doesn't matter now what you felt during the incident, but what they did. (Even if you believe you were in the right during the exchange, this exercise should demonstrate to you why they reacted the way they did, and perhaps make it easier to understand.)

Time for another quick break state. What will you watch on TV tonight?

Now, it's time to try for the third position, the observer. Picture the same event again but this time you are a neutral observer, looking down at the event. What does it look like now? What can you learn from this perspective that you didn't notice before?

Stop and take another pause. Now you're going to go back to positions one and two and see if anything has changed in your viewpoint (or the other person's) considering the above. What have you learned from it, and how are things different now?

Perhaps you had an argument with a friend in the pub. You were convinced he was the one in the wrong – of course, you got defensive when he criticised you in that way – but he stood his ground when you argued back.

It was so black and white, wasn't it? But now, perhaps you are starting to see shades of grey. Having viewed the incident as a neutral observer, you can admit that maybe your mate simply made a joke that backfired. After all, you were engaging in jokey banter all night.

As an observer, you watched as you both drank one or two more pints that was probably advisable, and you noticed how slurred your words became. You spotted your attention beginning to wane until your mate *'insulted you'*. Then suddenly you riled up and reacted with hostility.

Your friend, also drunk, raised his hackles in response. You can sense his anger and refusal to back down. Viewing the incident from his viewpoint, you now know why – you can feel his shock and disappointment that you would think so little of him that you would turn on him when he was simply continuing the banter.

Suddenly the event was a simple joke taken badly and blown out of all proportion by the two of you. You should both apologize. And well done, you have experienced empathy and understanding of another person's feelings. Now go and telephone your mate!

You can use this technique as often as you need to gain perspective on another person's feelings and actions.

When Empathy is Too Much

I've always considered myself to be empathetic, but I noticed that when I became a mother, my empathy levels ratcheted up a notch. Reading about children coming to any sort of harm would upset me, just imagining what that child's mother must be going through. I could almost feel the other mother's pain by imagining how I would feel if it happened to me. At times I felt it so acutely that I had to stop watching television news or reading similar stories in the newspaper.

That's another side to empathy – to be able to use it effectively, you need to be able to recognize and feel other people's emotions without adopting them yourself. You need to create emotional boundaries. Remember that you are only responsible for your own emotions and not others. Appreciate where their feelings are coming from, understand them and show empathy, but make sure to maintain self-control in emotional or stressful situations.

Improving Your Social Skills

Here we come to the final component of Emotional Intelligence, social skills. It's no coincidence that the most successful people in life have strong interpersonal skills, allowing them to negotiate, inspire, nurture relationships and work well with others.

Social skills are broad, of course, and when we talk about them in Emotional Intelligence terms, we mean the skill the understand, appreciate, handle and influence other people's emotions. Taken to extremes, this can be sinister and manipulative, but it can also be as simple as smiling at someone because you know it will make them smile back and improve their mood.

Consider it this way: Emotional Intelligence begins with recognizing your own emotions (self-awareness), learning how to control them (self-regulation), using them to achieve your goals (motivation) and then moving onto understanding the feelings of others (empathy) and using them to influence others (social skills). Our five EQ skills.

Social skills, therefore, in the Emotional Intelligence sense, includes the following factors:

- **Persuading and influencing**

- **Communication**

- **Conflict management**

- **Leadership**

- **Building rapport**

- **Change management**

- **Team-working**

Let's have a look at those in a bit more detail.

Persuasion and Influencing: enthusing others and winning them over, getting their support for your proposed plan of action. People high in Emotional Intelligence with strong influencing skills can read the emotional currents in a situation and tailor their communication to appeal to those involved.

How to Persuade and Influence

People with poor persuasion skills often try to achieve their aims by nagging or coercion – neither approach is likely to work in the longer term. A better approach is to encourage others to buy into your idea and want to do it your way.

Think of the fable of the sun and the wind. Both tried to *'persuade'* a man to take his coat off to win a competition. The wind blew and howled but the man only held onto his coat even tighter. The sun shone gently and within minutes the man took his coat off.

What can we learn from this? You can't really force someone to do something they don't want to do. The key to persuasion is to make them want the same thing that you want, and then they are more likely to do it.

How can you do this? Persuasion is a skill like any other in Emotional Intelligence and you can learn to hone it. In his book **Persuasion IQ: The 10 Skills You Need to Get Exactly What You Want**, Kurt Mortensen suggests there are several things people like about successful persuaders. These include being reliable, taking responsibility, sincerity, keeping promises, knowing and believing in their subject, being entertaining and providing solutions that work.

Successful persuaders tend to have high self-esteem and the confidence to believe they will succeed, and, critically, are strong in Emotional Intelligence. The latter is particularly useful when it comes to understanding what your audience thinks. Here you'll need to use your active listening and empathy skills, honed above. You will also need to be organized (do your homework, know your audience and your subject) and have strong communication skills to get your point across.

Communication Skills

Communication skills are a key component of Emotional Intelligence. You need to be able to listen to others and share your thoughts and feelings effectively. Pretty much everything we've talked about in this book so far touches on communication, so I'm not going to delve too deeply here, but let me just say that good communicators tend to:

- Listen well, see our section on active listening above.

- Don't allow problems or difficult issues to fester and grow but tackle them head on

- Want to hear genuine feedback and not only good news; they are prepared to hear about any problems

- Notice and act upon emotional cues, ensuring their message is appropriate.

Follow these tips – and the numerous other ones mentioned in this book – and you will improve your communication skills to no end.

Conflict Management

Another aspect of strong social skills is the ability to manage conflict, both at home and in the workplace. Conflict can often seem to come out of thin air, can't it, and if you're one of those people who prefers to ignore it, well, stop! Let's face it, most conflict doesn't miraculously go away. It festers and grows until something breaks, often relationships.

A good conflict manager will bring the disagreement out into the open, encourage the sharing of emotions and open discussion, reduce any hidden issues, aid both parties in recognizing each other's feelings and encourage them to recognize logical positions. They will try to seek win-win solutions, where both parties feel they have earned something from the exchange.

Tips for Handling Conflict

Probably the easiest model for handling conflict is the straightforward model below:

Describe the situation + Express your feelings + Ask for what you would like done

A couple of quick pointers:

If you're an active participant in the disagreement, take the time to cool down before tackling the problem. Vent if you need to, rant too, talk to a friend, but identify and deal with your emotions first. If someone around you is heated, take the time to calm them down first. Do this before you email your boss back or remind your significant other that you care for them before complaining about something.

Address the problem when you are both calm. The first thing you should do is to identify what the conflict is and make sure you and the other person (or the interested parties, if you're the mediator) agree on what the problem is. This is where describing the situation in our model above comes in. You'd be amazed how many times two people in a conflict can disagree on the cause or the problems arising from it.

Ideally propose solutions that are mutually beneficial (the win-win I talked about earlier) and be sympathetic if the other person is unwilling to concede certain things (though stand firm on your own issues too).

Try to end on a cooperative note, even if you can't agree on all points. Demonstrate to your boss or co-worker, for instance, that you want to work towards the same goal even if you disagree on how to get there. Let your wife, husband or significant other know that you will try to work on the issues he or she has raised, even if you can't agree to them all. Relationships, whether at home or in business, work best when the people involved believe they are on the same page, working towards the same goals.

I followed the model above with two of my team when conflicts arose at work. Both seemed to get on ok while I was in the office, but when I left – and my second-in-command deputized for me – communication and team work broke down. Both complained about the other, yet I knew that both were at the top of their game, so what happened when I was out of the office?

The first time it happened I tried to deal with it independently, speaking to the two of them separately, but it happened again. Soon both started sniping at each other, and I knew I couldn't allow it to go on any further. I worked off-site at our second site a lot and relied on Nigel to keep the team productive in my absence.

I called a meeting with the pair of them, warning them ahead of time that we were going to deal with the conflict in a professional and calm manner with no raised voices.

I set out the game plan from the start. Lacey, the most junior, would go first as she was the one who effectively had the complaint which was the way she was treated by my deputy when I wasn't in the room. She would have the opportunity to explain the situation and the conflict as she saw it and express her feelings, plus to say what she would like to see done differently. I made the point again that no one would be attacked, and we would deal with the disagreement calmly.

I also made sure to tell Nigel, my deputy, in front of Lacey, that he should listen to Lacey, consider if he agreed with the situation as she laid it out, and if not, to express his own view of the problem calmly and again without attacking. I stressed that he should apologize only if he felt he had done something wrong, but that he shouldn't be defensive and should be open to cooperation.

Lacey described the situation as she saw it. Effectively, it came down to Nigel being overzealous with his deputy role, 'bossing' the team about unnecessarily, but also in part doing the job that he was hired to do. (The team were about to move to a different position in the media empire we worked in, and Nigel had been hired to get them ready for a more fast-paced pressured role).

Nigel listened to Lacey's complaints, and was genuinely stunned by some of the examples that she gave of his behavior. Giving Nigel props, he admitted he hadn't realized that some of his actions could be construed in the way that they had and apologized for making Lacey feel that she couldn't be trusted with her work. That had never been his intention.

As per my instructions, however, he refused to apologize for being 'tough' on the team and pushing them to do better, pointing out that was why he was brought in. To do the hard job when I couldn't be in the office. As a mediator, I explained his role to Lacey more fully.

Lacey listened and appreciated the distinction but did point out that Nigel was like two different people – when he was deputizing and when he wasn't. The conflict confused the team, and they never knew 'which' Nigel they were getting. The jovial Nigel who liked to joke and be one of the team, or the buttoned-up 'boss' Nigel who micromanaged and never felt like anything was good enough.

Nigel, of course, hadn't realized he acted any differently during those moments in charge and I hadn't been around to see them. Faced with specific examples from Lacey, however, he accepted the point was well made and pledged to find a happier, medium ground. He was open to change but assertive enough to point out that he was still in charge when deputizing and wouldn't apologize for pushing the team when he felt it was needed.

Lacey respected that, and indeed I could see her respect for Nigel grow from that day on. She left the meeting happy that she had been listened to.

Subsequently, Nigel and I worked on his issues, specifically his confusion over his role when I was and wasn't in the office. When I was there to lead the team, for instance, where did he stand? We helped him to find a position of authority that didn't ebb and flow according to the situation each day.

Nigel and Lacey never had any issues after that, in fact, they became close friends in the office as well as outside of it. That meeting, while challenging as a mediator and even more daunting as a participant, was the best conflict management tool we could have used.

The idea in any conflict management situation is to be assertive without being aggressive. Indeed, assertiveness is probably the most important skill in conflict management. Active listening is also crucial to ensure you understand the positions of those involved in the conflict, whether you are the mediator or an active participant.

Finally, you will need the ability to recognize emotions in others (and ideally be able to point out to others when the emotions are fine to express or when they are inappropriate. *Empathy is also an extremely beneficial skill.*

Leadership Skills

We have a whole chapter coming up on leadership skills, so I'm not going to say much here apart from to note that leadership skills and Emotional Intelligence are inextricably linked. A good leader will have strong Emotional Intelligence skills and the ability to influence people and take others with them.

Building Rapport

Another way of saying building rapport is to talk about building bonds with people. This skill leads to better relationships at home, at work and in life in general. People who are great at building rapport tend to be strong networkers with an enviable ability to build and maintain contacts and connections. They may also have many friends at work. Rapport is all about being interested in people. More on this later in the book

Change Management

People who operate as change managers or catalysts are essentially able to make change happen without alienating everyone around them by making it an exciting opportunity rather than a threat. They challenge the status quo, lead from the front and remove barriers to change.

Team Working

We all know people that are great at team-work, and who seem to thrive working in partnership with others. We're also likely to know others that would much prefer to work alone. Team working – *collaboration, cooperation, commitment* – is a key social skill in Emotional Intelligence.

How to be a Team Player

Good team players collaborate and share ideas, fostering a cooperative climate. They often seek out potential team working opportunities and having good team players helps to lift the entire team to a higher level. You don't have to be in a leadership position to encourage good team-work.

The key is to think of the relationships and team dynamics as just as important as the task at hand; the result isn't the be all and end all. Forging a team identity and encouraging commitment will ensure future projects succeed, so don't destroy the team to achieve one single aim.

A Final Comment on Social Skills

I've said it before, but it is worth repeating. While social skills may demonstrate a person's effective Emotional Intelligence, it doesn't start or end there. Emotional Intelligence is a cycle, with the individual at its heart. Only those people who can understand and regulate their emotions are able to work well with others, using empathy and self-motivation to achieve their goals.

No man is an island; we all need other people at some point or another, and our ability to relate to them, our social skills, directly influences how successful, happy and content we are at home and beyond.

I've suggested some tips to hone your social skills above but let me give you a couple of generic pointers as well.

Choose One Skill

Deciding to improve your social skills can seem daunting, so start small: choose one specific social skill that you would like to develop to give you a focus. Daniel Goleman recommends identifying someone who is very good at the skill you want to hone and watching them. Observe how they act and control their emotions, before applying that knowledge to yourself.

Body Language

We're going to talk about body language in more depth later in the book, but for now be aware that the words you use aren't the only message you are sending to others. It has been said that non-verbal communication – *body language, eye contact, tone of voice* – accounts for as much as 93% of all communication and the actual content of your words only 7%.

Network

It's a traditional option but one of the best ways to practice your social skills – and yes, practice is important – is to attend local networking events. Such events usually give you a shared reason for attending, which gives you a starting point for any conversation.

Get Out There

It sounds so simple to say you should get out there and socialize, but it is the very best way to develop your social acumen. Joining a network or group beyond your normal social circle is a good start. Try and practice the suggestions contained in this book and your EQ skills should improve significantly.

Chapter 8: Learn from the Habits of Emotionally Intelligent People

Every Star Wars fan knows that Yoda has all the answers. That little green alien with the big ears may talk funny, but what he says can often be quite profound.

Bear with me here if you're not a Star Wars fan but in *The Empire Strikes Back*, for instance, Yoda displays the strength of the Force by lifting a spaceship from the swamp.

"I don't believe it," mutters Luke. *"That is why you fail,"* retorts Yoda.

The canny little dude has a good point. Neuroscience shows that confidence is critical to success.

Believing in yourself and your abilities helps to pave the way to achieving your goals and never giving up, and it's a skill that you can learn when boosting your Emotional Intelligence. Confidence is simply an emotion like any other, and if we know anything about EQ by now, it's that it all revolves around managing your emotions.

I've collated this tell-tale list highlighting the habits of Emotionally Intelligent people from my research and the tips peppering this book. It's always good to have them in one place. Practice what they preach. By doing so you'll create new neural pathways that will soon become habit in your own life.

And if you don't feel it quite yet, well you know what they say: *'fake it 'til you make it'*.

The 10 Habits of Emotionally Intelligent People (and What They Won't Do)

Be Positive

It's easy to watch the news on TV and be overwhelmed with war, attacks, illnesses, failing economies, natural disasters and more. But Emotionally Intelligent people only focus on the things which they can control, namely their effort and attention. It doesn't mean that they don't care about everything else, just that they must draw a line to stay optimistic. Studies show time and time again that optimists perform better at work and are physically and psychologically stronger and healthier than pessimists.

To achieve this, you must stop negative thoughts and self-talk in its tracks. The more you dwell on negative thoughts, the more power they have over you. Write down any negative thoughts you have and look at them with a calm eye – chances are they are not facts but fears or worries that have never come true, so refuse to let them control your behavior.

Remember: you can't prevent yourself from feeling emotions, but you can control how you react to them.

Help yourself to stay positive by also refusing to hang around negative people.

Use an Extensive Emotional Vocabulary

As I've already mentioned in this book, experts suggest only 36% of people can accurately identify their emotions as they occur. Unlabelled emotions can be misunderstood, and lead to irrational choices and poor reactions. People with high EQs understand their emotions, helping to master them; this includes knowing how to describe them in detail. The more specific the word, the better. Recognising that you feel *'anxious'*, for instance, helps you to work out its source better than if you could only describe yourself as feeling *'bad'*.

Be Assertive

While talking about conflict management in our last chapter, I mentioned that the key was to be assertive without being aggressive. Emotionally Intelligent people know how to balance empathy, manners and kindness with assertiveness and establishing boundaries. They stay balanced when cross and avoid the aggressive or passive behavior typified by their none-EQ counterparts. Their tact allows them to deal with toxic people without offending anyone. Emotionally Intelligence people are assertive enough to lead and set a direction without waiting for other people to follow or give them permission. They don't ask *'should I?'* but instead think *'why wouldn't I?'*

Don't Judge

Emotionally Intelligent people don't judge others; they don't need to put others down to make themselves feel good. They are confident enough not to compare themselves to other people, and their power of empathy ensures they care.

Be the Master of your Own Happiness

I said above that Emotionally Intelligent people don't need to compare themselves to others. If you don't hang on other people's opinions of you, no-one else can take away your happiness or sense of achievement when accomplishing something important. No-one else can limit your joy. Your self-worth instead comes from within.

People with high EQs know what makes them happy and work hard to ensure they carry this happiness into their work and life. Doing so helps them stave off stress.

Be Accountable

Emotionally Intelligent people are confident enough to be accountable for their actions, no matter whether making excuses would be an easier option. They care more about the result than they do their ego.

I said earlier that Emotionally Intelligent people focus on the things they can control, which is why they don't blame the things that they can't. The good news is that people are far more likely to remember the steps you took to correct a problem, than they are the fact that you may have caused it in the first place.

What You Should NOT Do!

Emotionally Intelligent people rarely exhibit the traits that I'm about to talk about, so if you do, it's time to take a step back and look at your behavior in the light of your EQ.

People with High EQs Don't Seek Attention or Praise

It's that confidence thing, again. When you are genuinely confident, you don't need to seek attention or praise because your self-worth comes from within. It's enough just to know that you have done your best; you don't need to be told so again and again. Don't confuse self-confidence with narcissism. The sort of confidence that is dependent on the praise of others isn't confidence at all, but vanity.

Equally, people with high EQs don't look for drama either. They may listen, be empathetic and offer advice to others, but they don't let other people's lives and dramas impact or rule their own.

People with High EQs Don't Hold Grudges

One thing that marks Emotionally Intelligent people out from the crowd is that they take steps to manage the stress that they feel and ensure it doesn't control them. Doing so allows them to maintain the balance that keeps their emotions in check and harmonious.

That's one reason why they don't hold grudges. Holding onto a grudge sends the body into the equivalent of a fight-or-flight stress response, which can wreak havoc on the body when it's not required. Remember the consequences of stress that we mentioned in chapter four? Stress has been linked to high blood pressure and heart disease. Letting go of a grudge not only helps your psychological health, but your physical health too.

People with High EQs Don't Procrastinate

Procrastination or putting things off is often a sign of fear, whether it's fear of change or failure (sometimes even success). Emotionally Intelligent and confident people believe in themselves and their goals, and don't sit around waiting for the right time to strike. They have confidence that their actions will bring about the result they want, and if the time isn't right, they make it right.

People with High EQs Don't Quit

Emotionally Intelligent people don't quit or give up when something goes wrong. They see challenges as obstacles to overcome. They are astute enough to know that failure can be a learning curve and, when faced with it, will work out what went wrong and what lessons could be learned before they try again.

To be truly Emotionally Intelligent and successful, you need to be prepared to make mistakes. A recent study at the College of William and Mary interviewed more than 800 entrepreneurs and found they had two critical factors in common: they refused to imagine failure and didn't care what other people thought of them. They saw failure as a necessary step towards reaching their goals and didn't stress about it.

It allowed them to learn from mistakes in the past but not to dwell on them, good advice for us all.

Chapter 9: How To Strengthen your Personal Relationships with Emotional Intelligence

Do you remember the statistic I quoted earlier in this book about the importance of Emotional Intelligence in marriage? I never warned you there'd be a test, did I?

Here it is again because it's a significant factoid and one that perfectly kicks off this chapter:

81% of marriages WILL fail if men refuse to share power. To share power, men need to be emotionally available and respect their other half, i.e. Emotionally Intelligent.

Yet only 35% of men ARE Emotionally Intelligent.

It's a conundrum, isn't it?

There have been bona fide studies proving the importance of Emotional Intelligence on interpersonal relationships. In one study, for instance, the participants rated their marital satisfaction higher if they also rated their marital partner higher for Emotional Intelligence. Another study demonstrated anticipated greater satisfaction in relationships with a partner of Emotional Intelligence.

A meta-analysis of six studies with more than 600 participants found a *'significant association'* between EQ and romantic relationship satisfaction. And it works both ways. The higher your own Emotional Intelligence, the more satisfied you will be in a romantic relationship, PLUS the higher your partner's EQ, the happier you will also be.

Isn't it worth beefing up your Emotional Intelligence for the pair of you, whether it's for your present or future Mr or Mrs?

The good news is that happy couples aren't necessarily better, luckier, richer or more intelligent than the rest of us; they are just in touch with their emotionally intelligent side.

As **Dr. John Gottman** himself, possibly the world's lead researcher on marriage, says: *"Happily married couples aren't smarter, richer, or more psychologically astute than others. But in their day-to-day lives, they have hit upon a dynamic that keeps their negative thoughts and feelings about each other (which all couples have) from overwhelming their positive ones. They have what I call an emotionally intelligent marriage."*

How does this manifest itself? According to Dr. Gottman, an emotionally intelligent marriage includes two partners who are committed to awareness of themselves and the other, and the ability to manage their own emotional state and its impact on the other partner. So, a classic trait of Emotional Intelligence.

To specify further, he adds: *"In the strongest marriages, husband and wife share a deep sense of meaning. They don't just 'get along'—they also support each other's hopes and aspirations and build a sense of purpose into their lives together."*

If marriage is a journey, you both know why you're in the car together and appreciate where you're going.

It's all the easier to live up to those marriage promises – to love, honor, respect and understand each other – if you are an emotionally intelligent couple. Not only can it help you avoid divorce or relationship breakdown, but as happily married people have been shown to live longer and healthier lives, it's great for your health too.

Emotional Intelligence isn't just crucial to love relationships. It's valuable for family and friends too, helping to sustain on-going positive relationships.

But if you're terrible at EQ, how *can* you improve? How can you be sure you're giving your significant other, friends and family the support they need?

Most of the time in close personal relationships, your actions will be natural, and you may not even be aware that you're using your EQ skills. If you're naturally low in Emotional Intelligence, however, it may take more purposeful thought and effort, but remember that EQ skills can be learned.

The truth is that you're more likely to be aware of your EQ skills (or lack thereof) if you don't have them.

Relationships

Does the next section sound like anyone you know, someone close to home perhaps? If you can't recognize them in yourself, has your partner or family complained about you suffering from any of the following? It's probably time to deal with it.

Out of Control Feelings: We all know by now that Emotionally Intelligent people can regulate their emotions. If your EQ needs work, you may be prone to lashing out in anger or giddy happiness for no real reason, or any other OTT emotional reaction.

Poor Friendships: How many close friendships do you have? Most people low in EQ struggle to maintain good relationships with co-workers and friends.

Can't Read Emotion: Do you often find yourself clueless about your partner's emotions, or blindsided by a reaction? You may be unable to read nonverbal cues, such as facial expressions or body language, or struggle to interpret tone of voice. So much of our communication is not said verbally. If you can't interpret that, you will struggle to make an emotional connection because you never quite know what the other person is thinking. The good news is that we have a section on non-verbal communication coming up just for you.

Poker Face: Can your partner tell what you're thinking and feeling, or do you have a poker face, unable to express your own emotion?

Are you Emotionally Inappropriate? Do you get angry over nothing, or fail to realize you are angering someone else? Perhaps you are inappropriate, such as telling jokes or laughing at a funeral. These can be signs that you struggle with the social side of emotional expression.

Can't Handle Sadness: Do you prefer to walk away from negative emotions or sadness, struggling to show empathy or support? A lack of empathy signals poor Emotional Intelligence. Do you find emotional movies leave you cold, for instance? Don't be fooled into thinking it's a male versus female thing; it's not. It's very possibly a sign that you have low EQ.

Overplay Logic: Logic has its place in relationships, but if you over-stress logic and cognition over emotions (and typically downplay the latter), it's a sign that you are subconsciously aware of your low EQ and trying to pretend it doesn't matter. Little tip: it does, for all the reasons I mentioned above.

Odd Interpretation of Emotions/ Conflicts: Have you been accused of over-reacting or having an odd reaction to conflict or emotions? Perhaps you acted hostile and defensive when there was no need. Often the root cause of this is confusion as opposed to malice, very possibly because of the above. Of course, when people don't understand that, you tend to withdraw even more.

Assuming you freely recognize your lack of Emotional Intelligence and appreciate the negative impact it is having on your personal life, what can you do about it? How can you go about developing your EQ in relationships in particular?

How to Develop your EQ in Relationships

I've already shared a lot of tips for improving your EQ in general earlier in the book. A lot of what I suggested there will help your EQ across the board, including with friends, family and significant other.

You may want to go back and re-read that chapter with your relationship in mind.

Now though I'm going to suggest a couple of further tips specific to romantic relationships. It's worth following even if you haven't found that special someone yet… who knows, perhaps becoming more in tune with your emotional side will help you land them!

Learn to Describe your Emotions

Yes, I know I've mentioned this a couple of times before, but it really is worth developing a strong emotional vocabulary in the context of relationships. Think of how you describe your emotions – happy, sad, angry… anything deeper? If you're sad, for instance, would you ever think of yourself as melancholy, depressed, grief-stricken, ill or nostalgic?

As we know by now, developing a wider emotional vocabulary allows you to go deeper and to correctly label your emotions, which in turn helps you to react accordingly. Having a wider emotional vocabulary encourages you to move past your first initial emotion, say anger, to determine exactly what lies beneath. Often our first instinctive emotional response seems like the most powerful, but it's not always the true story.

Say you have an argument with your wife. You feel and recognize your first emotion, anger. Would you ordinarily stop there? Now that you're seeking a stronger Emotional Intelligence, you should push past the anger to find what you're really feeling – could it be hurt, jealous, anxious, worried, embarrassed, ashamed?

Being hurt, for instance, feels very different to being angry, doesn't it? Or perhaps you're ashamed because you couldn't give your wife what she needed from you? Each emotion carries a different weight and influences how you relate to your partner, helping to make your relationship more genuine. Imagine if you'd just stopped at anger? You would understand a lot less.

Don't forget. While your first emotional reaction may seem the most powerful, it may also be the least honest.

Work on Relationship Awareness

The key to Emotional Intelligence is to be aware of, and in control of, our own emotions, while also recognizing emotions in others. Every single one of us needs something from our significant other, whether it's love, trust, support, affirmation.

Of course, what we need from the other changes as we age, our relationship grows, our circumstances alter etc.

How confident are you that you know exactly what your wife or husband needs from you? What *'emotional nutrients'* do they need that would feed your relationship? *(If the word 'nutrients' is confusing to you, consider emotional needs instead. What emotional needs does your wife need you to address?)*

The easiest way to find out is to ask. Ask your partner to write down the three most important emotional needs or *'nutrients'* that they have and want from your relationship. Write your own list independently. Swap and discuss how you can make sure the relationship or marriage can meet both lists.

Tackle Emotional Contagion

After reading even the first chapter of this book, you'll know that emotions can impact performance, and that's also true of marriage. Anxiety or anger can impact a relationship negatively, while more positive emotions such as confidence help to make the marriage productive.

Think back to Dr. John Gottman's advice at the beginning of this chapter. He said that the happiest couples were the ones who managed to keep their negative thoughts about each other from overwhelming their positive ones.

So, how can you do that? First, by recognizing that anger begets anger. Or, to put it another way, couples really can catch emotions from one another. If one partner is depressed, angry or anxious, the other partner will feel the same pressures. You can literally infect each other. It's called emotional contagion.

Research tells us that depression in a spouse often leads to depression in the partner; children raised by people with depression are more likely to be diagnosed with it too. The same is true for other emotions such as anger and anxiety.

Who is more likely to be susceptible to emotional contagion? Often women socialized to attend to the needs of the people around them. Ditto people who are strongly emotional and empathetic and who value connectivity over independence. Does that sound like your wife? Perhaps you fell in love with her because she understands far more about your emotions than you do. Better make sure you're not exposing her to negative contagions.

The good news is that positive emotions can be 'caught' too. Positivity, enthusiasm and confidence can lift a marriage and imbue both partners with a healthier outlook on the relationship and life in general.

Being Emotionally Intelligent – aware of your emotions and able to regulate them – is one of the most effective ways to avoid negative emotional contagion and to keep perspective.

The results might show themselves in something as simple as not shouting back at your wife if she shouts at you first or snapping at your husband when he snaps. It can mean the difference between feeling anxious in reaction to your partner's anxiety over household bills, for instance, or maintaining calm.

In short, it means that at least one person in the marriage can keep emotional perspective and steer the relationship through the choppy waters.

How To Understand Body Language

There's a formula that's often bandied around when we start to talk about body language and non-verbal communication – the **55/38/7** rule. It's a percentage formula that demonstrates how much is communicated when you're NOT speaking. Yes, that's right. People communicate even when they're *not* talking.

The 7% of the formula represents how much of communication is spoken. Your words, no matter how carefully you choose them, only account for 7% of all communication. Both liberating and daunting, isn't it?

In total, so the formula goes:

55% of all communication comes from body language

38% from tone of voice

7% actual words spoken.

That's the theory and has been since two studies combined formulas way back in 1967. Of course, there has been some dispute with the exact figures and it's fair to point out that such a simple theory can't possibly apply to every situation. But, experts agree, it's a pretty good ballpark and it really does emphasize the importance of body language.

Understanding someone's body language can tell you so much about a person, but what if you just weren't born knowing the cues? What if it all simply passes you by, and you fail to notice your wife is angry despite saying she's not, or your son is lying to you when he promises not to have a party this weekend? Can you learn how to recognize body language?

Let me tell you a little story. I was sat minding my own business in a local coffee shop recently *(meaning I was people watching, fascinated by their interactions)*. A young couple walked in and sat next to me, arguing all the while. I politely tried to ignore them *(ok, not really)* but they made it hard. The argument seemed to stem from the fact that the boyfriend had communicated with an ex-girlfriend, a fact he was trying hard to pretend didn't mean anything. Of course, his body language gave him away.

He tried so hard to convince his girlfriend with logic but was oblivious to what his body language and tone of voice – defensive, mock offended, *'caught like a rabbit in headlights'* – really revealed. Of course, we don't see our own body language so it's often hard to be sure if it's failing our intentions.

His girlfriend, of course, a woman of obvious Emotional Intelligence, saw straight through him, but for some reason either decided to accept his protestations or was saving them up to use against him later. Finally, she calmed down and her hapless and low EQ boyfriend thought that was the end of it. They sat in silence – communicating volumes to anyone who cared to look – and he thought he'd got away with it.

When they left, he tried to seal the deal with a hug. He was happy that she acquiesced, but her body language – stiff as a plank of wood, refusing to make eye contact – should have told him that he really shouldn't touch her.

I tell you, he was so busted. The next time I saw her in the same café, she was alone. I never did ask what happened to the boyfriend, but I can guess.

You see, if you're so blind to body language, you miss out on so much.

What is Body Language?

Before we go any further, let's just reiterate what we mean by body language as it's an all-encompassing term.

It's everything from eye contact *(or lack of)*, gestures, facial expressions, posture, space *(do they invade yours?)*, and touch *(a weak handshake versus a bearhug, for example)*.

Did You Know: Facial expressions are universal. They are the same across cultures for happiness, sadness, fear, shock and disgust etc. The same is *NOT* true of other forms of non-verbal communication, such as gestures and body language, so be careful!

Uses of Body Language

According to **The Importance of Effective Communication** by Edward G. Wertheim, body language can be used to underline or complement a verbal message *(think of a pat on the back when congratulating someone),* or to repeat what they say wholeheartedly. When it matches the spoken words, it increases trust and rapport between people.

Body language can, and often is, used instead of words – eye contact can communicate much more than words alone, don't you think? And it can also contradict what someone is trying to convey with words.

The kicker about that last point – research studies show that if your body language contradicts your spoken word, people are much more likely to believe the former. Not to mention distrust you. If you can read body language well, it's a built-in lie detector.

Body language can't really be faked. Unless you're a master manipulator and 'on' all the time, your true intentions will slip out, whether it's thanks to a gesture, a touch, an eye-roll or some other little clue.

How to Recognize Body Language

There are far more clues to body language than we can possibly talk about in one chapter – entire books have been written on it, after all. However, there are a few steps that you can take to make yourself more open and effective at interpreting non-verbal communication. They include:

Managing stress

When you're stressed, you are much more likely to miss the nonverbal signs that other people are putting out there. You'll be prone to misreading events and handling personal conversations poorly. Learning to manage stress is a key component of becoming emotionally intelligent, and it's important for effective communication too. If you're stressed by a discussion, take a time-out. Regain your emotional equilibrium before you say or do something you'll regret. Remember your emotions are contagious, as we talked about above.

Work on recognizing your emotions

Being aware of your and other people's emotions and how they influence you is a fundamental part of Emotional Intelligence and the purpose of this book. It's also a key component of recognizing body language, so there's a bonus! If you need to, re-read the tips in chapter seven and eight again and again until you feel ready.

Look for inconsistencies

Possibly one of the best tips for reading body language that I can give you is to look for inconsistencies between what someone says and what their nonverbal communication suggests. Ideally it should reinforce their words. If someone is saying yes while shaking their head no, that's something to be wary off, for instance. A word to the wise, however – don't try to evaluate every single non-verbal signal that you receive; it will make your head explode. People naturally consider all the clues given during a conversation to gain an overall impression of whether their words, tone of voice and body language are consistent or inconsistent with what is being said.

Pay attention to your instincts

Gut feeling is important, don't dismiss it. If you suspect someone isn't being truthful, you may be subconsciously picking up on a conflict between verbal and nonverbal clues.

If in doubt, ask

If someone's body language seems to contradict their spoken word – and it's not a potentially dangerous situation – feel free to ask for clarification. Don't get frustrated. Say something like, *'You said X and Y, but your body language suggests you think differently. Can you help me to understand?'* Just be careful not to do it aggressively or in an adversarial manner.

Well done on wanting to improve your EQ and your knowledge of body language to strengthen your relationships with your nearest and dearest. Next, we're going to look at how you can use your Emotional Intelligence to boost your success at work!

Chapter 10: Using Emotional Intelligence to Improve Success at Work

"In a high-IQ job pool, soft skills like discipline, drive and empathy mark those who emerge as outstanding"
Daniel Goleman

In today's technological global workforce, you could be forgiven for thinking that *'soft skills'* such as those advocated by Emotional Intelligence are becoming less important. After all, computers have little need of confidence, teamwork, communication skills, positive attitude…all the things improved by a strong EQ.

The self- check-out tills at the supermarket, for instance, certainly don't demonstrate empathy, do they?

Ok, it's important not to over-react in Emotional Intelligence, so I'll dial it down and look at the actual evidence… and it's good news. You see, the truth is that honing your EQ skills, especially your social skills, can give you an edge in a competitive environment, making you stand out from the rest of the workforce.

You are, in fact, less likely to be replaced by a machine if you can master your social skills.

According to Harvard economist **David Deming**, social skills is a growing area within the workplace. He studied workplace tasks from 1980 to 2012 and discovered that while the number of technical and analytical tasks remained the same or even declined, tasks needing social skills grew by 24%.

As Deming says in his paper, **The Growing Importance of Social Skills in the Labor Market** *"What explains the growing importance of social skills in the labor market? One reason is that computers are still very poor at simulating human interaction. Reading the minds of others and reacting is an unconscious process, and skill in social settings has evolved in humans over thousands of years.*

Human interaction in the workplace involves team production, with workers playing off of each other's strengths and adapting flexibly to changing circumstances. Such non-routine interaction is at the heart of the human advantage over machines."

Emotional Intelligence, therefore, can make a tremendous difference to your job prospects and success.

Experts theorize that EQ is responsible for nearly 60% of your job performance and can boost your pay packet by around $30,000 a year. It can also bring significant advantages for your employer too – a salesman or woman with high EQ can potentially sell twice as much as one with a low one. That's partly because people are prepared to buy from people they like and trust, even if it means buying an inferior product at a higher price.

If that doesn't persuade you of the importance of Emotional Intelligence in the workplace, don't forget that research concludes 90% of top performers tend to have high EQs.

In contrast, according to the Center for Creative Leadership *"75% of careers are derailed for reasons related to emotional competencies, including inability to handle interpersonal problems; unsatisfactory team leadership during times of difficulty or conflict; or inability to adapt to change or elicit trust."*

This basically means they estimate that three-quarters of careers are disrupted because of an inability to demonstrate effective Emotional Intelligence.

There will be many circumstances that you will come across in your working life that would no doubt benefit from Emotional Intelligence. Let's look at how your EQ could help in a few typical situations right now.

Using Emotional Intelligence To Handle a Bully Boss

You're lucky if you've never experienced a bully boss; I have, and it's not pleasant. You'll often find the bully is low in Emotional

Intelligence and can't handle his or her stress or know how to talk to people effectively. Perhaps he or she feels threatened by others or inferior in some way and doesn't know how to handle or address those feelings.

Whatever the reason, being on the other side of repeated workplace bullying can not only ruin your working hours but erode your quality of life as well.

So how would you address a bully boss using your Emotional Intelligence? David Goleman himself suggests this response:

Self-awareness: Here's where you work hard to recognize your physical and emotional reaction to the abuse. Does your heart race and red mist descend when your boss humiliates you? Does your vision narrow if you feel intimidated? Recognising your body's physical and emotional cues to what Goleman calls an *'amygdala hijack'* – when the rational part of the brain is pushed aside in favor of the emotional *'Fight, Flight, Freeze or Faint'* response – is the first step to controlling it.

Self-regulation: Honing your Emotional Intelligence will help you to stop the amygdala hijack in its tracks. You may need to walk away, take a breather, consider relaxation or meditation techniques (these will be easier to access the more you practice), but calming down and allowing the rational brain back in will help you choose how best to react.

Empathy: Are you the only one being bullied in the workplace? Chances are you're not. Use your empathy skills to pick up on cues, even if no one else has dared to speak about it yet. Look for someone in the office who seems less impacted by the bullying. What do they do to handle it? Can you learn from them how to keep calm?

Social Skills: Use your empathy and self-awareness to remind co-workers that bullying shouldn't be a normal part of your day. Together you are stronger.

Using Emotional Intelligence To Avoid Emotional Contagion

'Every time we allow someone to move us with anger, we teach them to be angry'
Barry Neil Kaufman

If you've read my previous chapter, you'll know all about emotional contagion – that one angry person can infect the mood of everyone around him. You can literally catch emotions like the flu. Emotional contagion can happen in a group, an organization or even one-to-one.

Our brains are wired to pick up and mirror emotions from other people automatically and unconsciously. Without realizing it, we notice social cues, such as facial expressions, which we then unwittingly copy in a form of non-verbal synchronicity. Think of a fast-paced conversation with a friend; the discussion can move so quickly precisely because of this harmony.

When you're instinctively reacting to negative cues, attitudes and behavior, however, it begins to infect you, turning you as depressed, angry or as anxious as the person you're mirroring.

In a group, the sender of emotions is usually the most emotionally expressive. If there are power differences within the group, it's usually the most powerful person in the room who sets the emotional tone for everyone else.

It's worth re-reading my comments on this in the previous chapter to learn how to withstand negative emotional contagion. But perhaps you don't want to reject it, perhaps you want to take advantage of it.

If you're the leader of the group, for instance, you can set a positive tone that others will pick up on and enhance their performance.

You really do have that much power. It's something to be aware of every time you enter a room. Use the Emotional Intelligence lessons you have learned in this book to be aware of, and regulate, your own emotions.

If your mood isn't useful to the team, change it, recommends Sigal Barsade, a researcher at the Wharton School of the University of Pennsylvania. Dr. Barsade, who specializes in emotional contagion, suggests one way to change your mood is to alter your facial expression, taking advantage of the *'facial feedback hypothesis'* – the notion that our facial expressions influence our emotions. Smile if you want to feel positive.

Using Emotional Intelligence To Cope with Toxic People

Toxic people deft logic, don't they? Some genuinely have no idea that they suck out the life, soul and motivation of the people around them, while others delight in creating chaos and strife. They are a source of stress that we're often just not prepared for. Whether it's the negativity, craziness, victim mentality or cruelty, we need effective strategies to deal with toxic people in the workplace.

A great deal of the threat that toxic people bring in the workplace is due to emotional contagion, the phenomenon I mentioned above. If you have a toxic worker spreading negativity, other people will slowly start to feel it too.

If you're the boss, you need to neutralize the toxicity, either by talking to the person concerned *(often they don't know how negatively they are being perceived) or* if the negativity is deliberate, by determining and discussing the source of the displeasure.

Other emotionally intelligent strategies to deal with toxic colleagues, whether co-workers or subordinates, include:

<u>Setting Limits</u>

You wouldn't inhale second-hand smoke all afternoon by sitting next to a smoker, would you, so why allow a complainer or negative person to wallow by your side all day. Set limits and refuse to get sucked in. Distance yourself when necessary, or otherwise ask them how they intend to fix the problem. That should at least change the direction of the conversation.

Stay Aware of your Emotions

You can't maintain an emotional distance without awareness or prevent someone from getting to you if you don't recognize that it is happening at the time. This is where the self-awareness inherent to Emotional Intelligence comes in. Use it, hone it. Smile and nod, if you need to, rather than allowing your buttons to be pushed.

Focus on Solutions, not Problems

I used to have a boss who wouldn't listen to problems if I couldn't also provide solutions. It was as annoying as Hell, but one way to encourage positivity. The thinking behind it is that whatever you focus your attention on will determine your emotional state. Don't focus on how problematic the toxic person is, instead concentrate on how you will handle him or her. It will give a sense of efficiency that will help to reduce stress and introduce positive emotions.

Limit your Caffeine

It might sound flip, but caffeine triggers adrenalin release, the source of the *'fight or flight'* stress mechanism. As we said above, this often sidesteps rational thought in favor of an instinctive response, but this is not a bear you're facing, it's just an angry colleague.

Get Enough Sleep

A good night's sleep can potentially be the best ally you have when it comes to dealing with stress, simply by helping your brain to recharge and wake up clear-headed. Trust me, you'll need that to deal with anyone toxic. Sleep deprivation raises the stress hormone all by itself, and reduces your attention, memory and all-important self-control as a result.

Using Emotional Intelligence To Motivate

According to Gallop research, only 13% of workers worldwide are *'engaged'* in their jobs, potentially bringing *'serious and potentially lasting repercussions for the global economy.'*

People who are demotivated underperform, walk out at the first opportunity and spread lethargy everywhere they go. In contrast, motivated employees are a third more productive and sell more than a third extra than their non-motivated counterparts, according to research from the University of California.

Motivated staff are also 87% less likely to quit, all things good for the bottom line.

'No one cares how much you know, until they know how much you care'
Theodore Roosevelt

There are many different forms of motivation, and what motivates one person may not work well on another. Some of the best motivators that I've seen focus on the social side of things… regular Friday after-work drinks, for instance; chocolate Wednesdays; monthly State of the Union meetings where team members could have their say, hear from other members of the company and have paid-for drinks afterwards. What could go wrong? *(Little tip: if you're the boss, try to avoid the very drunken and belligerent team members who will inevitably regret their outburst the next morning. Deal with their issues without alcohol.)*

Of course, alcohol doesn't have to be included, but getting the team together, encouraging them to like one another socially, to form close bonds, is an important element of an emotionally intelligent workplace.

At my old workplace, there was a history of distrust and dislike between editorial and advertising. Projects between the two used to be fraught with suspicion, defensiveness and frustration, and rarely flowed as well as they could.

After a particularly intense meeting which amounted to little more than an all-out argument, I walked out of the room to see the *'always together'* advertising representative holding her head in her hands. Her body language showed me exactly how frustrated – and fed-up – she was. I felt sorry for her. Perhaps we in editorial were a touch too defensive, honed from numerous meetings like this one, and she no doubt had lots of pressure from above.

I suggested we meet over coffee to discuss the joint project again in lesser emotive circumstances. We did, and coffee became a glass of wine as we thrashed out an agreement that we could both live with. That project went without a hitch and if we ever had a problem afterwards, we discussed it over lunch or wine, but we were just two people. It was time to ease tensions throughout the departments.

We spearheaded an informal *'getting to know you'* plan, encouraging our teams to chat to *'the other side'* during our monthly State of the Union post-drinks party. Slowly, each side began to see the other as people, not adversaries, as colleagues they even liked and could have fun with. And here's a secret – it's much harder to get annoyed with someone you got drunk with the night before!

Managers are directly responsible for the motivation of their employees, so assuming you're a leader, how else can you use Emotional Intelligence to boost team motivation?

Offer Compassion

Leaders with Emotional Intelligence care about their employees and want the organization to do so as well. They don't just think of the bottom line. They are not afraid of other people's emotions and treat everyone with consideration.

Communicate Effectively

The tips and techniques behind Emotional Intelligence – keeping emotions in check, listening without judgment etc. – inevitably lend themselves to effective communication. A leader who shares their strategy or vision with the team will encourage motivation, ensure everyone is on the same page and forge a more efficient workplace.

Treat Yourself and Others with Respect

An emotionally intelligent manager or leader practices self-respect, which is reflected to the people he or she manages. If you respect yourself, you will rarely speak disrespectfully to anyone, no matter what the provocation. Demeaning people is never the answer.

Connect with Employees on an Emotional Level

Emotionally intelligent leaders are comfortable with, and understand, the people around them, helping them to forge close relationships. They naturally find people interesting and their authenticity and genuine interest helps to build rapport and trust.

Cold and calculating bosses, on the other hand, are often too detached from their employees, and dictatorships rarely succeed long-term in a company. Employees will not go the extra mile for someone who can't even address them with warmth. Note that being a 'leader with a heart' doesn't mean you're a pushover.

Lead with Confidence and Intuition

In your leadership career, there will inevitably be times of stress and crisis, when things just aren't going right. As a confident emotionally intelligent leader, people will look to you for behavioral cues and you need to ensure you don't overreact or become overwhelmed. The self-confidence to make decisions based on intuition honed through accumulated wisdom will inspire others. Logic can't be the only deciding factor.

Provide More Autonomy

The best emotionally intelligent leaders build trust with their team, meaning they should be comfortable delegating tasks and giving people autonomy. A self-aware manager should know his or her own strengths and weaknesses and recognize the opposite qualities in others. Offering autonomy to deserving employees demonstrate trust and value, and boosts morale and motivation.

Develop People's Careers

One of the key reasons people quit a job is because they just can't see a future there anymore. Any organization that doesn't help to develop their people's careers will suffer from a talent drain which, once begun, can become contagious and demotivational.

Emotional Intelligence, however, can break the cycle. Investing time to help team members establish future goals and finding opportunities to achieve within the company can be highly motivational for employees.

Thanks for reading this book so far. I hope you're finding the tips helpful. Learning to develop your Emotional Intelligence really can change every aspect of your life, as I hope I've demonstrated by now. We're nearly at the end of this book but it would be remiss of me to sign off without a word of warning… you'll find it in my final chapter on the Hidden Dangers of Emotional Intelligence.

Chapter 11: The Hidden Dangers of Emotional Intelligence

I've spent the whole of this book enthusing about Emotional Intelligence and cheerleading its many, many positive qualities. You know by now, for instance, how being EQ-savvy can strengthen your relationships, balance your emotions and help you thrive at work.

Marriages are stronger if the partners have high EQs and spouses are happier; meanwhile, children with high EQ parents are more likely to form suitable peer relationships, have a balanced outlook on life and reach their academic potential.

Emotional Intelligence at work helps you to be a team player and an effective leader, to achieve success, earn more money, sell more and make the workplace a more enjoyable place to be.

Emotional Intelligence can be a truly beautiful thing when it's used for the right reasons.

But here's the rub. Emotional Intelligence, by its very nature, is morally neutral, and I would be remiss in finishing this book without first warning you of its hidden danger… ___manipulation.___ You see, Emotional Intelligence can be used for good or evil, depending on the person utilizing it.

Here's a real-life example. If I put Martin Luther King Jr and Adolf Hitler in the same sentence, much less suggested they had something in common, you might be offended. But the truth is that they did share one skill… **Emotional Intelligence**.

They both used Emotional Intelligence to get their message across… one for good, one for evil.

The 'Dark Side' of Emotional Intelligence

When Martin Luther King Jr presented his dream, he not only kept his own feelings in check, but he used language that sparked emotions in others, moving them to action. His electrifying message – *"a perfectly balanced outcry of reason and emotion, of anger and hope,"* according to his speechwriter Clarence Jones – was a classic example of Emotional Intelligence used for good.

The problem is that once someone is talented at Emotional Intelligence, it becomes easier to manipulate others… something Adolf Hitler understood only too well.

Hitler spent years workshopping his gestures, facial expressions and body language – often in front of a mirror – to become a captivating public speaker… and a master manipulator. He recognized the power of emotions and used it, horrifically, against his subjects.

As best-selling author and psychologist Adam Grant writes in The Atlantic, *"When you're good at controlling your own emotions, you can disguise your true feelings. When you know what others are feeling, you can tug at their heartstrings and motivate them to act against their own best interests."*

Jochen Menges, a University of Cambridge professor, nicknamed this the *'awestruck effect'*. In his research paper, he argued that charismatic leaders could both stir the hearts of their followers and overwhelm them with emotion that they were too intimidated to express.

This impaired their cognitive processing ability, meaning that they often failed to evaluate the actual message delivered by the charismatic leader. They lost their capacity to reason. The result? They endorsed leaders with little scrutiny.

This *'dark side'* could be true of charismatic leadership whether the leader was moral or immoral, argued Menges. However, you don't have to imagine how much devastation such power could cause in the wrong hands – we've already seen it in Adolf Hitler's.

Emotional Intelligence and Narcissism

Much of the manipulation in such circumstances comes from people with personality *'issues'* already.

'There's a reason narcissists don't learn from mistakes and that's because they never get past the first step which is admitting that they made one.'
Jeffrey Kluger

Studies examining the influence of high Emotional Intelligence, for instance, have found a disturbing correlation with narcissism, extreme self-centredness which often comes at someone else's expense.

Highly emotionally intelligent narcissists, for instance, can use their knowledge of emotions to trick you into feeling a certain way, or behaving in a particular manner. They manipulate you into doing whatever they want, usually with some end game for themselves.

One study, Is There a Dark Intelligence?, concluded that "The utilization of EI skills for the emotional manipulation of others is facilitated by dark personalities (namely, narcissists and psychopaths). To the extent that EI can be and is used for malicious purposes (e.g., deception, exploitation, harm of others), a "dark intelligence" may be formed by those who use EI as a tool to a self-serving and manipulative end."

Note that narcissism can easily be mistaken by a casual observer for a social disorder such as Asperger's Syndrome. The difference is that someone with Asperger's may not understand what you are feeling, whereas a narcissist simply wouldn't care. Their own personal goals are more important.

Identifying Manipulation

Unfortunately, the workplace offers plenty of opportunity for people with high Emotional Intelligence to be devious and self-serving. Such behavior could include spreading rumours and gossip, distorting or blocking information and focusing on *'strategically important targets'*, such as supervisors, rivals and subordinates.

Your high EQ co-worker may manipulate you by playing on fear to spur you into action or by showing you just one side of the story.

They may take advantage of your good mood to demand something, or act with reciprocity, asking for something only after they have supposedly done you a good turn, knowing you'll find it harder to say no.

Beware too people who ask lots of questions and want to get to know you without revealing anything of themselves. They could be looking for weaknesses. Finally, if someone wants to manipulate you they may speak quickly or use jargon to confuse; force your hand by issuing unreasonable timescales or give you the silent treatment.

Of course, not everyone with high Emotional Intelligence aims to manipulate or gain the upper hand; often EQ is simply used to help achieve goals.

It does bring home, however, the fact that Emotional Intelligence isn't necessarily benevolent.

A 2010 journal paper, **Strategic Use of Emotional Intelligence in Organizational Settings: Exploring the Dark Side**, argued that EQ should be divorced from its association with *'desirable moral qualities'*.

Instead, author Martin Kilduff, a University College London professor, states: *"We have shown that the strategic disguise of one's own emotions and the manipulation of others' emotions for strategic ends are behaviors evident not only on Shakespeare's stage but also in the officers and corridors where power and influence are traded."*

The best way to tackle such manipulation is to be aware of it, to hone your own Emotional Intelligence so that you can recognize the emotional landscape and any attempt to take advantage of it.

But how do you make sure you don't misuse your new Emotional Intelligence skills? Is it possible to manipulate without knowing it?

Good questions and yes, it is possible to manipulate without deliberate intent, but as a rule, if your intentions are pure, so will your actions be.

If you're in doubt, concentrate on your empathy. Empathetic concern for others should overwrite any self-concern, and act as an antidote to the 'dark side'. As does being aware of the moral implications of Emotional Intelligence, which you now are thanks to this chapter.

A Final Word...

Emotions play a huge part in our lives, both at home and at work. We are not robots, and nor should we strive to be. Emotional Intelligence really can transform lives for the better, despite the warnings in this chapter.

If you're a husband or wife struggling to connect to your significant other, or a parent worried about the impact of your emotional shortcomings on your child, learning about those emotions and understanding how to control them can improve your relationships significantly.

Developing empathy and *'walking a mile in someone's shoes'* will help you to appreciate the people around you, while social skills will boost your ability to be close to them.

Careers are won and lost in the workplace, thanks to Emotional Intelligence. Learning how to boost yours will help you to reach for success.

The main career-related reasons for failure include difficulty handling change, poor interpersonal relationships, and being unable to work well in a team. Enhancing your EQ will help to banish all of those, whether it comes naturally to you or not.

And that's the one thought I want to leave you with:

Great (emotionally intelligent) leaders aren't always born; sometimes they are made.

Ditto great husbands, wives, partners, friends and parents.

Emotional Intelligence is a skill, and it is one that anyone can learn if you put your mind to it.

Good luck!

Thank you for checking out my book.
I sincerely hope you got value from it. I hope it allows you to make important changes in your life.

If you liked this book could you possibly take 60 seconds to write a quick review on Amazon?

Reviews are a vital way for books to get more exposure and help to spread the message.
Thank you. Your support is very much appreciated.

Emily Porter

9269R00077

Printed in Great Britain
by Amazon